Fresh Ways with
Pork

COVER
A roast loin of pork is sliced to reveal its stuffing of spinach, mushrooms and chestnuts. THis dish combines the stuffing from the recipe on page 52 with the instructions for preparing and cooking a boned loin of pork in the recipe on page 50. The accompanying gravy is made from wine and stock stirred into the juices of the roasting tin.

TIME-LIFE BOOKS

EUROPEAN EDITOR: Ellen Phillips
Design Director: Ed Skyner
Director of Editorial Resources: Louise Tulip
Chief Sub-Editor: Ilse Gray.

ISBN 0 7054 2010 8
TIME-LIFE is a trademark of Time Warner Inc. U.S.A.

HEALTHY HOME COOKING

SERIES EDITOR: Jackie Matthews
Picture Editor: Mark Karras
Studio Stylist: Liz Hodgson
Editorial Assistant: Eugénie Romer

Editorial Staff for *Fresh Ways with Pork*
Editor: Charles Boyle
Researcher: Sebastian Thomas
Designer: Paul Reeves
Sub-Editor: Wendy Gibbons

Editorial Production
Chief: Maureen Kelly
Assistant: Samantha Hill
Editorial Department: Theresa John, Debra Lelliott

THE CONTRIBUTORS

JOANNA BLYTHMAN is an amateur cook and recipe writer who owns a specialist food shop in Edinburgh.

SILVIJA DAVIDSON studied at Leith's School of Food and Wine and specializes in the development of recipes from Latvia.

JEREMY ROUND, a former deputy editor of the *Good Food Guide,* is food correspondent of *The Independent* and the author of a forthcoming book on Turkish regional cookery.

HILARY WALDEN is a food technologist. She has written numerous books and articles on all aspects of cookery.

The following also contributed recipes to this volume: Maddalena Bonino, Jo Chalmers, Caroline Conran, Antony Kwok, Norma MacMillan, Cecilia Norman, Emma Ogden, Lynn Rutherford, Louise Steele, Sebastian Thomas, Jeni Wright.

THE COOKS

The recipes in this book were cooked for photography by Pat Alburey, Jacki Baxter, Allyson Birch, Nicola Diggins, Antony Kwok, Dolly Meers, Lyn Rutherford, Michelle Thompson. *Studio Assistant:* Rita Walters.

NUTRITION CONSULTANT

PATRICIA JUDD trained as a dietician and worked in hospital practice before returning to university to obtain her MSc and PhD degrees. Since then she has lectured in Nutrition and Dietetics at London University.

Nutritional analyses for *Fresh Ways with Pork* were derived from McCance and Widdowson's *The Composition of Food* by A. A. Paul and D. A. T. Southgate, and other current data.

This volume is one of a series of illustrated cookery books that emphasize the preparation of healthy dishes for today's weight-conscious, nutrition-minded eaters.

Fresh Ways with Pork

BY

THE EDITORS OF TIME-LIFE BOOKS

TIME-LIFE BOOKS/AMSTERDAM

Contents

2 *Balancing the Flavours* 65

Vinegar Pork with Garlic

Pork Char-Shiu

Light Gumbo

Pork and Spinach Terrine

Golden Casserole

Stuffed Pig's Trotters

The Humble Provider

The food of the common people rather than of kings, pork has for centuries been a dietary mainstay for millions worldwide. The reasons have much to do with economy: the pig is easy to raise, being omnivorous and requiring little land for grazing; and almost every part of its carcass can be eaten. However, two associated misconceptions — that the pig is by nature an unclean animal and that its meat is only for those who cannot afford better fare — have tended in the past to obscure pork's virtues: its distinctive flavour and its high level of nutritional benefits.

Our standard image of the pig — stocky, snub-nosed, its rounded bulk finished with the merest doodle of a tail — is itself somewhat out-of-date and misleading. This awkward, overloaded beast was first developed by progressive European stockbreeders of the 18th century, who aimed to produce an animal that would satisfy the high-energy dietary requirements of an active population. Since then, of course,

our lifestyles have in general become more sedentary and our eating habits have changed accordingly. Today's pig is bred more for its lean meat than for its fat. Rich in protein, minerals and B vitamins — especially thiamine (vitamin B1), which is essential for the release of energy from carbohydrate — lean, fresh pork has much to contribute to a healthy diet.

Pork, fat and cholesterol

A pig's carcass contains about 32 per cent fat, and after all surface fat has been trimmed from fresh pork the lean meat that remains contains an average of 7 per cent fat (compared with 9 per cent in lean lamb and 4.5 per cent in lean beef). It is worth emphasizing that the strictures of modern nutritionists are directed not against fat itself, but against the quantity of fat in our diet — and even if it were possible to eliminate fat altogether, this goal would not be desirable. For fat is an essential nutrient, it provides certain fat-soluble vitamins and helps the body to absorb these; it contains essential fatty acids that the body cannot produce itself but which are converted by the body into the basic

material of cell membranes; and it is the most concentrated source of energy available. In addition, fat contributes to flavour and palatability and, because it takes longer to digest than protein and carbohydrate, it is chiefly responsible for that comfortable feeling of satisfaction that comes after eating well.

Fat becomes culpable only when we eat too much of it — which, in the Western world, we tend to do. About 40 per cent of our caloric intake is accounted for by fat, compared with about 10 per cent in developing countries, and studies have shown that this high proportion is not only more than we need, but is associated with the high incidence of both obesity and coronary heart disease in the m affluent societies.

Closely linked with the issue of fat in the diet is that of the notorious compound cholesterol, which is present in pork in noticeable quantities. Excess cholesterol deposited within the walls of blood vessels can lead to circulatory problems and hence to arterial and heart disease; but the problem is not so simple as this connection implies. Present in all animal tissue, cholesterol is an organic fatty substance that is needed for the fluidity of our cell membranes and for the synthesis of certain hormones and vitamin D. The amount of cholesterol we take in with our food is normally far less than what is produced by the body itself, and does not by itself raise the cholesterol in our blood to unacceptable levels. The villain of the piece is really saturated fat, which stimulates the body's own synthesis of cholesterol. (In contrast, polyunsaturated fats, present in certain plant and vegetable oils, can actually reduce cholesterol by aiding the body's mechanisms for getting rid of it.) For this reason, while it is sensible to be aware of the cholesterol levels in our diet and to eat only occasionally cholesterol-rich foods such as liver and kidneys, the main precaution we should take against raising the amount of cholesterol in our blood is to reduce our intake of fat, and especially of saturated fat.

What this means for the health-conscious cook is not that pork should be avoided, but rather that it should be cooked in new ways that capitalize on its benefits. The amounts of fat and cholesterol in each dish should be kept within reasonable limits, and the same also applies to salt: several studies have shown that for some people excessive sodium intake may be linked with high blood pressure and strokes. It is the purpose of this book to show how these limits can be achieved without sacrifice to texture and taste.

Choosing the right ingredients

All the recipes in this book have been carefully developed to produce dishes that are both healthy in terms of their nutritional contents and attractive, flavourful and satisfying. To conform with these guidelines, the recipes concentrate on those cuts of pork that contain least fat and sodium. The cuts most frequently called for are loin and fillet, both of which derive from the upper part of the carcass in which the proportion of fat to lean meat is relatively low. Belly and many of the other cuts *(see page 10)* are generally too high in fat. Liver, brains and kidneys are too high in cholesterol to be eaten more than occasionally, while cured meats — bacon, gammon and ham — are too high in sodium. The lean cuts are inevitably more expensive than the fatty cuts, but by restricting individual portions to no more than 90 g (3 oz) of cooked meat (based on 125 g/4 oz of raw meat) and combining the meat with other appetizing ingredients that enhance its flavour, you can make each dish sufficiently economical to form part of an ordinary weekday meal.

Lovers of traditional pork cookery will be relieved to learn that not all of the cheaper cuts are outlawed, nor are charcuterie products and the special flavour of cured meat forbidden absolutely to the healthy eater. Meat from the neck end or the hand and spring, trimmed of all visible fat, is used in some of the stews, and in certain recipes you can substitute cheaper cuts of pork for the more expensive ones specified in the ingredients list — as long as you make allowance for the increased fat content when planning other dishes in the day's menu. The book includes recipes for a low-calorie terrine and for sausages made from lean minced pork with light, nutritious ingredients such as apples or potato in place of additional fat. Even ham, liver and kidneys — in moderate amounts, and cooked with due care — feature as primary ingredients.

The choice of ingredients that are cooked with the meat is in part determined by the need to cut down on fat and cholesterol. High-cholesterol dairy products such as cream and cheese should be used sparingly, or replaced with low-fat yogurt or *fromage frais*. There remains a vast range of healthy ingredients for you to choose from, many of them traditionally associated with pork in different national cuisines — for example, apples and cider in British dishes, fresh and dried fruits in French dishes, red and white cabbage in central European dishes and chili peppers in Mexican dishes. Each ingredient brings its own nutritional benefits to the assembled dish: beans and dried fruits, for example, add fibre, while fresh fruits and vegetables are valuable sources of vitamins. A comparable range of herbs and spices, many of them also associated with particular cuisines, can be used to give piquancy to the meat in place of salt.

The list of ingredients at the head of each recipe in this book begins with the pork and continues with the remaining ingredients in order of use. For clarity, the ingredients for a self-sufficient part of the dish — such as a marinade, sauce or pastry dough — may be listed separately. Both metric and imperial weights and volumes are given for each ingredient; the two sets of figures are not exact equivalents, and should not be mixed for the same recipe. Many of the recipes conclude with a suggested accompaniment to the main dish.

Cooking pork the healthy way

The nutritional value of a dish is affected not only by the choice of raw ingredients but by the technique used to cook them. The recipes in this book are divided into four chapters according to the cooking methods employed: the first two chapters cover dry cooking (sautés, grills, roasts) and moist cooking (stews, braises, and poached and steamed dishes). The third chapter contains a variety of less easily categorized methods, and the final chapter is devoted to cooking with a microwave oven. The introduction to each chapter includes hints and suggestions appropriate to the recipes that follow, but there are a number of points about cooking pork in a healthy way that should be born in mind whichever cooking method you employ.

To keep down calories and fat content, all surface fat should be trimmed off the meat with a sharp knife before the pork is cooked. For the same reason, the meat should be cooked in heavy-bottomed or non-stick pots or pans using the absolute minimum amount of cooking oil.

Fat that melts out of the meat during cooking should be discarded, by a process known as cleansing or degreasing. Use a soup ladle or a large, shallow spoon to skim off the fat that rises to the surface of a liquid in which the meat is being cooked; if necessary, tilt the pan or set it half off the heat so that the fat will collect on the still side of the pan. Small amounts of fat that remain can be removed with paper towels: lay a corner or strip of paper towel directly on the fat, then immediately lift it away.

To prevent the meat from drying out during cooking — a role traditionally accomplished by the fat in the meat itself or by basting or larding with additional fat — a number of strategies are available. These include filling the meat with a moist stuffing that bastes the meat from within, and tenderizing the meat before it is cooked by pounding it flat or steeping it in a marinade. Typically, marinades contain an acidic liquid — such as wine, lemon juice or vinegar — which softens the meat fibres and allows the other flavouring ingredients to penetrate; because acids react with metal to produce an unpleasant taste, the pork should always be left to marinate in a glass, enamel or other non-reactive dish.

In dry cooking, the meat is first subjected to a high heat to brown the surface, and then the heat is reduced to allow the centre of the meat to cook through. The purpose of the initial searing is twofold: firstly, the outside of the meat undergoes complex chemical changes known as "browning reactions" that produce an intense, highly appetizing flavour; and secondly, a crust is formed on the surface of the meat that helps to seal in its juices. To add colour and flavour, meat that is to be braised or poached may also be browned over high heat or in the oven before the liquid is added.

One major health hazard associated with pork cookery is trichinosis, caused by the ingestion of undercooked pork infected with tiny worms — *trichinae* — that burrow into the muscle of the pig and live in the human intestines. Invisible to the naked eye and capable of surviving both refrigeration and the heat of smoking, the worms can be destroyed only by thorough cooking. Although the number of pigs affected is extremely low, it is still worth taking elementary precautions: do not taste uncooked pork — even to test a raw sausage mixture for flavour — and cook all pork to an internal temperature of at least 75°C (170°F). (This does not mean that pork should be overcooked — the temperature given is no more than is required for the meat to be palatable.) Test small pieces of meat such as chops by pricking them with a skewer: if the juices that flow out are pink, the meat must be cooked longer. Larger pieces should be tested by inserting a cooking thermometer into the thickest part of the meat, avoiding any bones.

Going back to nature

Most of the pork cuts that are now sold in butchers' shops and supermarkets come from animals that have been raised intensively on factory-like farms. In recent years an increasing number of people — including both farmers and consumers — have become concerned about the possible side-effects of this type of farming.

Whereas sheep are generally raised outdoors and cattle are kept outdoors for at least the summer months, most pigs are housed for all their lives in buildings where light and temperature are strictly controlled. They are routinely injected with antibiotics and have growth-promoting agents added to their feed, which itself derives from land treated with nitrates and pesticides. The humans, therefore, who ultimately consume the meat of these animals ingest resistant strains of bacteria and chemi-cal residues which can cause illnesses and allergic reactions.

In Europe and America there are now associations of farmers dedicated to organic cultivation and the raising of animals by traditional methods. While exploiting the benefits of scientific progress where appropriate — for example, in the use of antibiotics to treat sick animals — these farmers do not use nitrogen, pesticides and other unnecessary chemicals, and they allow their animals to range freely in natural conditions. They take pains to spare the animals stress and bruising while being transported and in the slaughterhouse.

Most of the farmers who adhere to the rules laid down by the various associations sell their produce by mail order or through specialist shops, and at present their meat constitutes a very small proportion of the total market. However, it is worth seeking out, for the sake of both health and flavour. Free-range pork costs more than meat from intensively reared pigs, but you are unlikely to regret the extra expense.

Buying and storing pork

Whether buying fresh pork from a specialist retailer such as those described above or from an ordinary butcher or supermarket, look for firm, odourless, fine-textured meat. The flesh should be pale and pinkish, the fat white, and the bones tinged with red. Most pigs are slaughtered at the relatively young age of six to seven months; coarse-textured flesh and white, hard bones usually indicate an older animal.

Like other meats, pork should be stored in the refrigerator at a temperature of between 2° and 6°C (35° and 43°F). Ideally, the meat should be laid on a rack over a plate and covered with an upturned bowl so that moisture is retained but air can circulate round the meat. Minced pork will keep for one or two days under these conditions, fresh pork for three to four days. Cooked meat and leftovers should be wrapped tightly in film or foil, and kept for no more than two days.

Freezing is not considered beneficial to pork: its young, tender meat tends to harden, and freezer burn — surface discoloration and loss of nutritive value caused by drying out at low temperatures — can occur more quickly than with most other meats. If you do wish to store pork in the freezer, first trim off all visible fat, which can reduce storage life. Wrap the trimmed meat tightly in vapour-proof film or aluminium foil to prevent freezer burn and to keep out oxygen (which causes fat to become rancid). Keep the pork at a temperature of -18°C (0°F) or lower. Under these conditions, pork will keep for between three and six months in the freezer. The meat can be transferred to the refrigerator one to two days before it is needed, to thaw gently; alternatively, it can be thawed in a microwave oven. It should be kept covered during thawing, and then cooked at once.

The Key to Better Eating

This book, like others in the Healthy Home Cooking series, presents an analysis of nutrients contained in a single serving of each dish, listed beside the recipe itself, as on the right. Approximate counts for calories, protein, cholesterol, total fat, saturated fat (the kind that increases the body's blood cholesterol) and sodium are given.

Healthy Home Cooking addresses the concerns of today's weight-conscious, health-minded cooks by providing recipes that take into account guidelines set by nutritionists. The secret of eating well, of course, has to do with maintaining a balance of foods in the diet; most of us consume too much sugar and salt, too much fat and too many calories, even too much protein.

Interpreting the chart

The chart below gives dietary guidelines for healthy men, women and children. Recommended figures vary from country to country, but the principles are the same everywhere. Here, the average daily amounts of calories and protein are from a report by the U.K. Department of Health and Social Security; the maximum advisable daily intake of fat is based on guidelines given by the National Advisory Committee on Nutrition Education (NACNE); those for cholesterol and sodium on upper limits suggested by the World Health Organization.

The volumes in the Healthy Home Cooking series do not purport to be diet books, nor do they focus on health foods. Rather, they express a commonsense approach to cooking that uses salt, sugar, cream, butter and oil in moderation while employing other ingredients that also provide flavour and satisfaction. Herbs, spices, aromatic vegetables, as well as fruits, peels, and juices, wines and vinegars are all used towards this end.

The recipes make few unusual demands. Naturally they call for fresh ingredients, offering substitutes when these are unavailable. (The substitute is not calculated in the nutrient analysis, however.) Most of the in-

---

Calories **250**
Protein **23g**
Cholesterol **70mg**
Total fat **11g**
Saturated fat **3g**
Sodium **185mg**

---

gredients can be found in any well-stocked supermarket; the occasional exception can be bought in speciality or ethnic shops. A glossary on pages 140-141 describes terms and ingredients that may be unfamiliar.

In Healthy Home Cooking's test kitchens, heavy-bottomed pots and pans are used to guard against burning the food whenever a small amount of oil is used, but non-stick pans could be utilized as well. Both safflower and virgin olive oil are favoured for sautéing. Safflower was chosen because it is the most highly polyunsaturated vegetable fat available in supermarkets, and polyunsaturated fats reduce blood cholesterol; if unobtainable, use sunflower oil, also high in polyunsaturated fats. Virgin olive oil has a fine fruity flavour lacking in the lesser grade known as "pure". In addition, it is — like all olive oil — high in monounsaturated fats,

which are thought not to increase blood cholesterol. When virgin olive oil is unavailable, "pure" may be substituted.

About cooking times

To help the cook plan ahead effectively, Healthy Home Cooking takes time into account in all of its recipes. While recognizing that everyone cooks at a different speed, and that stoves and ovens differ in temperatures, the series provides approximate "working" and "total" times for every dish. Working time stands for the actual minutes spent on preparation; total time includes unattended cooking time, as well as time devoted to marinating, steeping or soaking. Since the recipes emphasize fresh foods, they may take a bit longer to prepare than "quick and easy" dishes that call for canned or packaged products, but the payoff in flavour and often in nutrition should compensate for the little extra time involved.

In order to simplify meal planning, most recipes list accompaniments. These are intended only as suggestions, however; cooks should let their imaginations be their guide and come up with their own ideas to achieve an appealing and sensible balance of foods.

Recommended Dietary Guidelines

		Average Daily Intake		Maximum Daily Intake			
		CALORIES	PROTEIN grams	CHOLESTEROL milligrams	TOTAL FAT grams	SATURATED FAT grams	SODIUM milligrams
Females	7-8	1900	47	300	80	32	2000*
	9-11	2050	51	300	77	35	2000
	12-17	2150	53	300	81	36	2000
	18-54	2150	54	300	81	36	2000
	54-74	1900	47	300	72	32	2000
Males	7-8	1980	49	300	80	33	2000
	9-11	2280	57	300	77	38	2000
	12-14	2640	66	300	99	44	2000
	15-17	2880	72	300	108	48	2000
	18-34	2900	72	300	109	48	2000
	35-64	2750	69	300	104	35	2000
	65-74	2400	60	300	91	40	2000

*(or 5g salt)

Techniques for Quality Cuts

For many of the dishes in this book, the cook's first task is preparing the meat — boning, trimming, slicing, mincing or flattening the pork according to the requirements of the specific recipe. Although no professional expertise is necessary, such tasks can be carried out most efficiently by following a logical sequence of steps. The techniques demonstrated on the opposite page and overleaf will help you to prepare successful dishes with the minimum of wastage.

Lean minced pork can be ordered specially from your butcher, but the only way to ensure a truly lean product with precisely the consistency you require is to prepare the meat yourself. This can be done with a mincing machine or a food processor, or by finely chopping by hand *(opposite page, above)*; the latter technique will retain more of the meat's juices. The meat shown in the demonstration is pork fillet, which is specified in a number of the recipes that call for lean mince, but neck-end, boned loin and certain other cheaper cuts can also be minced in the same way after they have been trimmed of fat.

The tender meat of the fillet makes it an appropriate cut for all of the dry cooking methods employed in Chapter 1. Sliced lengthwise and flattened out with a wooden mallet *(opposite page, below)*, the fillet can be rolled round a prepared filling and then roasted in the oven; or if the fillet is cut into equal-sized slices which are then tenderized by beating *(page 12, above)*, it yields medallions of pork for frying or grilling.

Chops and loin steaks are usually fried or grilled, and provide a quick, easy meal for a family lunch or supper. Several of the recipes in this book, however, show you how to transform these simple cuts into more special dishes by stuffing them with apple slices *(page 19)*, fennel bulb leaves *(page 95)*, pine-nuts and rice *(page 126)* and a number of other fillings. Cutting out the cavity in the chop that holds the stuffing requires only a few deft turns with a sharp knife *(page 12, below)*.

Boning a whole loin of pork may appear to be a more ambitious procedure, but this too requires only a quickly learned dexterity with a sharp knife. The middle loin cut shown on page 13 contains both the kidney and the fillet; once removed, these can be cooked separately. The rib bones — which must be cut free from the meat and snapped off — and the vertebrae that make up the spinal column can be used to make a meat stock. The boned loin may be rolled round a stuffing — such as the puréed broad beans and yogurt mixture on page 50 — and roasted, or it can be braised in the oven — as in pork cooked like game *(page 73)*, where the meat is first marinated in a mixture of wine, herbs and juniper berries.

In all the techniques shown, good-quality kitchen knives with sharpened blades are essential. Hone the blades on a sharpening steel before using them, and wipe them clean after every use. To protect the work surfaces in your kitchen, always place the meat that is to be cut or chopped on a wooden board.

A Guide to Pork Cuts

This diagram identifies the primal cuts into which the pig's carcass is divided and lists the main retail cuts derived from them. The proportion of lean meat to fat is highest in the loin and chump end *(coloured areas)*, the sources of the pork used in most of the recipes.

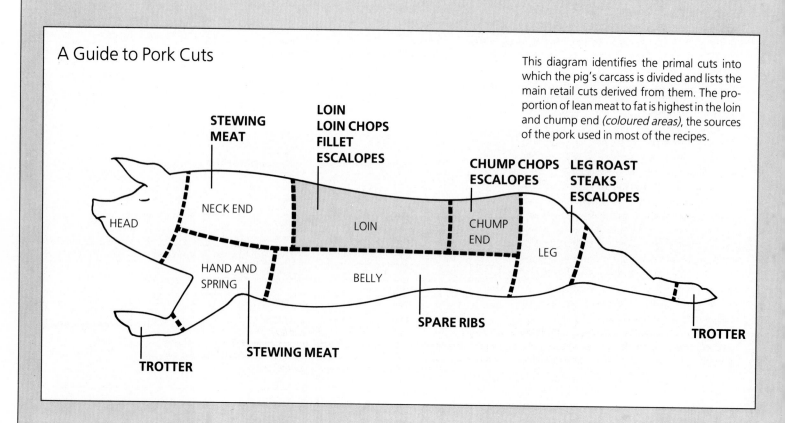

STEWING MEAT

LOIN
LOIN CHOPS
FILLET
ESCALOPES

CHUMP CHOPS
ESCALOPES

LEG ROAST
STEAKS
ESCALOPES

NECK END

HEAD

LOIN

CHUMP END

LEG

HAND AND SPRING

BELLY

TROTTER

STEWING MEAT

SPARE RIBS

TROTTER

Trimming and Mincing a Fillet

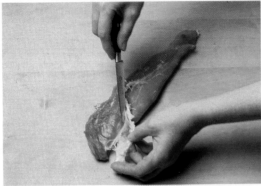 

1 *PEELING OFF THE MEMBRANE. Lift up an edge of fatty membrane with your fingers and peel it away from the fillet, lightly pressing a knife blade down the underside of the membrane and against the meat to help separate the membrane. Discard each strip as it comes free.*

2 *CUTTING INTO STRIPS. Lay the fillet on a cutting surface, one short end towards you and, using a long, sharp knife, cut it lengthwise into strips about 8 mm (⅓ inch) wide. Cut across the strips to make 8 mm cubes.*

3 *MINCING. Spread the cubes out evenly on the cutting surface. Use a matched pair of sharp, heavy knives to chop the meat finely; let the blades fall alternately on to the meat, using your wrists to control the knives as if beating a drum (above, left). From time to time, slide the blade of one knife under the meat and fold it back on itself (above, right). Continue chopping and folding until the fillet is a consistent mass of finely chopped meat.*

Flattening a Fillet

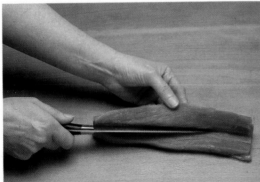 

1 *SLICING OPEN THE FILLET. Trim off all visible fat and membrane (above, Step 1). Place your free hand on top of the fillet to steady it and use a long, sharp knife to cut the fillet lengthwise to a depth of about 4 cm (1½ inches). Lift the upper section and deepen the lengthwise cut to within about 8 mm (⅓ inch) of the opposite side.*

2 *FLATTENING THE FILLET. Open out the fillet into a rectangular shape and lay it on a sheet of plastic film. Cover the fillet with a second sheet of plastic film. Using the flat, wide side of a wooden mallet, beat out the fillet to the thickness required for the recipe.*

Making Medallions from Pork Fillet

1 *CUTTING ON THE SLANT. Trim off all visible fat and membrane from the fillet with a sharp knife (page 11, above). Working from the thick end and holding the knife at an angle of about 45 degrees to the fillet, cut off the number of slices required.*

2 *BEATING OUT MEDALLIONS. Place the slices on a sheet of plastic film, then lay a second sheet of film on top. Using the flat, wide side of a wooden mallet, pound the slices firmly to the size and thickness required.*

Preparing and Stuffing a Chop

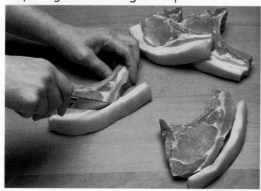

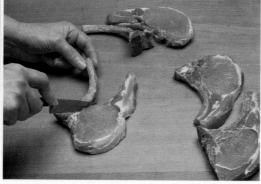

1 *TRIMMING OFF THE FAT. Working from the narrow end of the chop, use a sharp knife to trim off the band of fat and rind. Take care not to cut into the flesh with the blade of the knife.*

2 *BONING THE CHOP. Again working from the narrow end of the chop, use the knife to separate the rib bone from the flesh, pulling away the bone with your free hand as you cut (above). At the thick end, use the point of the blade to cut and twist away the bone.*

3 *PREPARING THE CAVITY. Cut a shallow slit about 4 cm (1½ inches) long in the rounded side of the chop (above). Press the knife blade deeper into the chop and work it backwards and forwards to hollow out a deep, wide cavity that extends almost to the edges of the meat.*

4 *STUFFING THE CHOP. Open up the slit in the rounded side of the chop with the fingers and thumb of your free hand, and fill the cavity with the prepared stuffing. Press the stuffing firmly into the chop to distribute it evenly.*

Boning a Loin

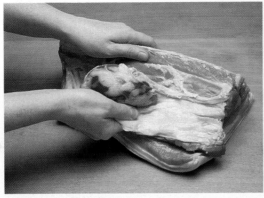

1 REMOVING THE KIDNEY. Set the loin rib side up on a cutting surface. Lift the kidney away from the ribs (above) and cut through the membrane that connects it to the loin. Trim off loose fat and membrane from the loin.

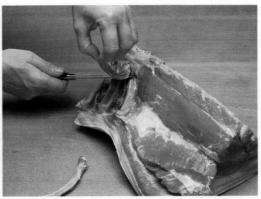

2 LOOSENING THE RIBS. To loosen each rib, first cut along both sides of the rib, taking care not to cut into the flesh any deeper than necessary. Then prise the rib upwards and cut underneath it towards the spine (above).

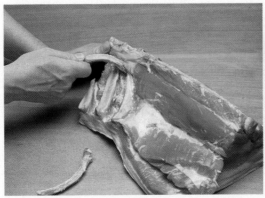

3 DETACHING THE RIBS. Holding the loin steady with your free hand, grip the end of the rib between your thumb and forefinger and twist it to break it away from the spine. If the bone is slippery, grip it with a paper towel. Remove the other ribs in the same way.

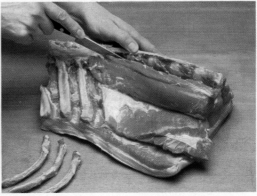

4 RELEASING THE FILLET. Keeping the knife blade close to the bone, cut along the spine to release the fillet (above). As the connective tissue is severed, the fillet will fall away from the spine.

5 LOOSENING THE SPINE. Feel with your fingers where the extensions of the vertebrae protrude into the flesh. Cut round and under the extensions with the tip of the knife to free them from the flesh.

6 CUTTING AWAY THE SPINE. To free the spine, work the knife blade underneath the spine along its entire length, using your other hand to pull the spine away from the flesh as you proceed.

1 Lean pork chops are marinated in a paste of yogurt, turmeric and Indian spices before being cooked under a hot grill (recipe, page 37)

Simple Succulence

Cooking by direct heat — or, in the case of sautéing, by the transfer of heat from the pan — is the simplest and oldest method of preparing fresh pork for the table. For sautéing and grilling, the meat must be thin enough to cook through before the surface burns — chops, escalopes, steaks and cubes or slices of meat cut from the loin are suitable candidates for these methods. For roasting, which cooks meat more slowly, larger cuts such as whole loin or fillet are more appropriate, but for all dry cooking methods you should select tender meat containing little connective tissue.

In traditional pork cookery, fat played an important role in keeping the meat moist during cooking — a roast, for example, might be basted with its own juices and liquid fat, a lean joint might be barded with fat or threaded with lardons, and cubes of meat might be alternated on skewers for grilling with pieces of fatty bacon. Because very little cooking oil is used in these recipes, and the meat itself is trimmed of surface fat before cooking, a certain amount of ingenuity is required to keep the meat from drying out.

To reduce the cooking time required, pork that is to be sautéed or grilled can first be tenderized by pounding with a mallet, or by steeping in a marinade. For Oriental stir-fried dishes, the meat is cut into thin strips that can be cooked through in as little as 15 seconds. In the recipe for crépinettes on page 56, the oval patties are wrapped in caul, a thin membrane of fat from the pig's stomach that melts and moistens the meat during cooking. For roasts, the meat may be stuffed with moist ingredients that release flavoursome juices during cooking. Or the meat may be roasted with a little liquid poured round it — wine, lemon juice and chopped tomatoes in the Cretan roast on page 58.

In many of the recipes, the caramelized deposits that remain on the base of the pan after the meat has been sautéed are incorporated into a sauce by deglazing the pan with a liquid such as wine, stock or fruit juice, and then simmering this liquid with additional ingredients. If the meat has first been marinated, the reserved marinade is often added to the pan at this stage. Reduced by rapid boiling or thickened with a little arrowroot, the sauce is poured round or over the meat on the serving dish. While this sauce is being prepared, the meat can be kept warm in a low oven in a dish covered with greaseproof paper.

After roasting, larger pieces of meat should be left to rest for about 10 minutes before serving. During dry cooking, the blood and juices in the meat tend to concentrate in the centre, and will run out if the meat is carved immediately; the resting time allows the juices to circulate evenly and the meat to become firm.

Tea Pork Chops with Two Purées

Serves 4
Working time: about 40 minutes
Total time: about 3 hours (includes marinating)

Calories **340**		
Protein 36g		

8	boneless middle-loin chops (about 125 g/4 oz each), trimmed of fat	8
8	shallots, finely chopped	8
12.5 cl	red wine	4 fl oz
45 cl	unsalted veal stock (recipe, page 139)	¾ pint
300 g	sweet potatoes	10 oz
350 g	broccoli florets	12 oz
90 g	fromage frais	3 oz
½ tsp	salt	½ tsp
	freshly ground black pepper	
Cardamom marinade		
5 tbsp	unsalted veal stock or water	5 tbsp
2½ tsp	strong Indian tea leaves	2½ tsp
32	cardamom pods	32
½	lemon, grated rind only	½
½ tsp	salt	½ tsp
	freshly ground black pepper	

Calories **340**
Protein **36g**
Cholesterol **70mg**
Total fat **11g**
Saturated fat **5g**
Sodium **310mg**

To prepare the marinade, bring the stock or water to the boil. Remove from the heat, add the tea leaves, cover and leave to infuse for 3 minutes. Strain the liquid into a bowl, add the cardamom pods, lemon rind, salt and some pepper. Cover and leave to cool for 20 to 30 minutes.

Remove the cardamom pods from the tea mixture and press them with the back of a spoon until they open; scrape out the seeds and crush them lightly with the spoon, then return both pods and seeds to the liquid. Place the pork in a large, shallow dish, pour the marinade over, cover with plastic film and leave in a cool place for 2 hours, turning the meat once.

About 30 minutes before the marinating is finished, sauté the shallots in a non-stick saucepan until transparent, then add the wine and simmer until the pan is almost dry. Pour in the stock, bring back to the boil and simmer to reduce by half — 15 to 20 minutes.

Remove the chops from the marinade and pat them dry with paper towels. Strain the marinade; reserve some of the cardamom pods for a garnish.

Add half of the strained marinade to the reduced sauce base, bring to the boil, then simmer to reduce to a light syrupy consistency. Add more of the marinade according to the consistency you prefer. Strain the sauce through a fine-meshed sieve and keep it warm.

In a dry non-stick frying pan, sear the meat over high heat for 2 minutes on each side. Reduce the heat and continue to cook for a further 10 minutes, turning once. Remove the meat from the pan and leave it in a low oven to rest for a few minutes.

Meanwhile, boil or steam the sweet potatoes and broccoli in separate saucepans until tender. Purée the

vegetables separately in a food processor or vegetable mill. Blend half of the *fromage frais* into each purée and add salt and pepper; pass the mixtures through a sieve if a smoother texture is preferred. If either of the purées appears too runny, cook it in a saucepan over low heat to thicken.

Transfer the purées to separate serving bowls. Place two chops on each diner's plate, pour a little sauce over and garnish with the reserved cardamom.

EDITOR'S NOTE: *Other vegetables of contrasting taste and colour may be used for the purées — for example, Brussels sprouts and swedes, or spinach and carrots.*

Chops with Redcurrant Sauce

Serves 4
Working (and total) time: about 20 minutes

Calories **245**	4	pork chops (125 to 150g/ 4½ to 5 oz each), trimmed of fat	4
Protein **29g**	500 g	redcurrants, washed	1 lb
Cholesterol **60mg**		freshly ground black pepper	
Total fat **9g**	½ tbsp	safflower oil	½ tbsp
Saturated fat **4g**	2½ tbsp	redcurrant or raspberry vinegar	2½ tbsp
Sodium **270mg**	2 tbsp	redcurrant jelly	2 tbsp
	½ tsp	salt	½ tsp

Reserve a few whole redcurrants for a garnish, and

pass the remainder through a sieve. Discard the contents of the sieve and reserve the sieved purée.

Season the meat on both sides with some pepper, rubbing it in with your fingers. Heat the oil in a heavy frying pan over high heat and, when it is smoking, add the chops. Brown them quickly on both sides and reduce the heat to very low. Continue cooking, turning occasionally, until the meat is firm but still springy when you press it with your finger — about 7 minutes. Remove the chops from the pan and keep them warm.

Deglaze the pan with the vinegar, and cook over high heat until the vinegar has almost evaporated. Add the redcurrant purée and jelly to the pan, and reduce for about 1 minute; add the salt. Serve the chops with the sauce and the reserved whole redcurrants spooned round them.

Stuffed Pork Chops with Calvados

Serves 4
Working time: about 30 minutes
Total time: about 45 minutes

Calories **375**
Protein **29g**
Cholesterol **70mg**
Total fat **14g**
Saturated fat **4g**
Sodium **270mg**

4	boneless pork chops (about 125 g/4 oz each), trimmed of fat	4
3	dessert apples	3
1 tbsp	finely chopped fresh thyme, or 1 tsp dried thyme	1 tbsp
	freshly ground black pepper	
3 tbsp	fresh lemon juice	3 tbsp
1½ tbsp	safflower oil	1½ tbsp
12.5 cl	calvados	4 fl oz
1½ tbsp	single cream	1½ tbsp
½ tsp	salt	½ tsp

Make a small incision in the side of each chop and carefully cut a pocket *(page 12)*. Peel, core and slice one apple finely, sprinkle half of the thyme over the slices and press them into the cavities in the chops. Season the chops with some pepper, rubbing it in with your fingers. Peel, core and slice the remaining apples, not so finely, and sprinkle with the lemon juice to prevent them from discolouring.

Heat half of the oil in a heavy or non-stick frying pan over high heat. When it is hot but not smoking, add the chops and brown for 1 minute on each side. Remove the pan from the heat and allow the chops to sizzle for another 3 minutes, turning once. Remove the chops from the pan and keep them warm.

Heat the remaining oil in the frying pan, and add the apples and the remaining thyme. Cook gently over medium heat until the apples are almost soft. Remove from the heat. Add the calvados and, when the sizzling has stopped, return to the heat and cook for 1 minute. Add the cream and allow to bubble up once. Replace the chops in the pan, pouring in any juices that have collected; add the salt, warm through and serve.

SUGGESTED ACCOMPANIMENT: *parslied carrots.*

EDITOR'S NOTE: *The softness of the fried apples should contrast pleasantly with the crunch of those inside the chops.*

Stir-Fried Pork and Squid

Serves 4
Working time: about 25 minutes
Total time: about 1 hour (includes marinating)

Calories **200**
Protein **23g**
Cholesterol **205g**
Total fat **10g**
Saturated fat **2g**
Sodium **320mg**

250 g	pork fillet, trimmed of fat and cut into thin strips	8 oz
250 g	squid, cut into thin strips	8 oz
1 tbsp	low-sodium soy sauce or shoyu	1 tbsp
1 tbsp	dry sherry	1 tbsp
16	spring onions	16
1 tsp	cornflour	1 tsp
4 tbsp	unsalted vegetable or chicken stock (recipes, page 139) or water	4 tbsp
1 tbsp	arachide or safflower oil	1 tbsp
1 tsp	sesame oil	1 tsp
2 tsp	finely chopped fresh ginger root	2 tsp

Put the strips of pork and squid in a non-reactive dish with the soy sauce and sherry, and leave to marinate for 45 minutes. Cut the spring onions in half and slice some of the green tops into julienne for a garnish. Remove the pork and squid from the marinade and set them aside. Mix the cornflour and the stock or water into the marinade.

Heat the oils together in a wok or heavy frying pan until they are hot but not smoking, add the ginger and stir-fry for 1 minute. Add the pork and squid and stir-fry for 4 minutes; then add the spring onions and cook for another 2 minutes. Pour in the marinade mixture, cook for a final minute, and serve at once, garnished with the spring onion julienne.

Stir-Fried Pork with Mange-Tout

Serves 2
Working time: about 30 minutes
Total time: about 50 minutes (includes marinating)

Calories **135**
Protein **14g**
Cholesterol **175mg**
Total fat **4g**
Saturated fat **2g**
Sodium **220mg**

250 g	pork fillet, trimmed of fat and cut into 5 mm (¼ inch) thick strips	8 oz
5	dried shiitake mushrooms, soaked in water for 20 to 30 minutes	5
12	baby sweetcorn	12
3	spring onions	3
2 tsp	safflower oil	2 tsp
1	garlic clove, crushed	1
1 cm	fresh ginger root, cut into fine julienne	½ inch
200 g	bamboo shoots, thinly sliced lengthwise	7 oz
200 g	mange-tout	7 oz
1 tsp	low-sodium soy sauce or shoyu	1 tsp
1 tsp	dry or medium-dry sherry	1 tsp
2 tbsp	unsalted veal stock (recipe, page 139) or water	2 tbsp
1 tsp	cornflour or potato flour, mixed with 4 tsp cold water	1 tsp
1	small carrot, sliced into fine julienne	1

Sherry marinade		
1 tsp	low-sodium soy sauce or shoyu	1 tsp
1 tsp	dry or medium-dry sherry	1 tsp
1 tsp	cornflour or potato flour	1 tsp
	white pepper	

To prepare the marinade, mix together the soy sauce, sherry, cornflour or potato flour and a little white pepper in a non-reactive dish. Add the pork strips and toss them well to coat them evenly, then leave to marinate for 15 to 20 minutes.

Meanwhile, strain the mushroom-soaking liquid and reserve it; squeeze the mushrooms dry and slice them thinly. Blanch the sweetcorn for 5 minutes in a pan of lightly salted boiling water with a squeeze of lemon juice added, then refresh them in cold water and drain. Shred the spring onions finely along the grain and put the strips in a bowl of iced water; when the strips have curled, drain them.

Heat 1 teaspoon of the oil in a wok or a large, deep frying pan until it is hot but not smoking, then stir-fry the pork strips over medium-high heat until they are light brown. Remove the pork strips from the wok and drain them in a sieve over a bowl.

Wipe the wok clean with paper towels, then heat the remaining oil until smoking and add the garlic. Discard the garlic when brown and add the ginger, bamboo shoots and mushrooms. Stir-fry for 3 minutes, then add the mange-tout and stir-fry for a further 3 minutes.

Reduce the heat and add the soy sauce, sherry, stock or water, reserved mushroom-soaking liquid and any meat juices from the pork strips. Increase the heat and cook for another 2 to 3 minutes; then add the cornflour mixture and stir until the sauce thickens and turns translucent. Add the pork strips and the sweetcorn to the wok and heat them through for 1 minute, then remove the wok from the heat and stir in the carrot julienne.

Serve the finished dish from the wok with the spring onion curls sprinkled over it.

SUGGESTED ACCOMPANIMENT: *plain boiled rice.*

Pork and Ginger Stir-Fry Salad

Serves 4
Working time: about 35 minutes
Total time: about 50 minutes

Calories **235**
Protein **23g**
Cholesterol **70mg**
Total fat **14g**
Saturated fat **4g**
Sodium **205mg**

500 g	pork fillet, trimmed of fat and cut into thin strips	1 lb
1 tbsp	sesame oil	1 tbsp
1	garlic clove, crushed	1
2.5 cm	piece fresh ginger root, finely chopped	1 inch
1 tsp	chili sauce	1 tsp
2 tbsp	low-sodium soy sauce or shoyu	2 tbsp
3	shallots, thinly sliced	3
⅛ tsp	five-spice powder	⅛ tsp
1 tbsp	safflower oil	1 tbsp
1	sweet red pepper, seeded, deribbed and cut into thin strips	1
Lettuce and bean sprout salad		
½	small red oakleaf lettuce, washed and dried	½
6	curly endive leaves, washed and dried	6
1	bunch watercress, washed, stems trimmed	1
4	Chinese cabbage leaves, washed, dried and shredded	4
4	spring onions, sliced diagonally	4
125 g	bean sprouts	4 oz

In a large, non-reactive bowl, mix the sesame oil with the garlic, ginger, chili sauce, soy sauce, shallots and five-spice powder. Add the pork strips and mix well. Cover and marinate for at least 15 minutes.

Meanwhile, prepare the salad. Arrange the oakleaf lettuce, curly endive leaves and watercress sprigs in a border round a serving dish. Mix the shredded Chinese cabbage with the spring onions and bean sprouts, and place the mixture in the centre of the dish.

Heat the safflower oil in a large heavy frying pan. Add the pork and its marinade, and cook over fairly high heat for about 4 minutes, stirring all the time. Add the red pepper strips and cook for a further 1 to 2 minutes, again stirring all the time. Pile the hot pork mixture over the prepared salad and serve at once.

Stir-Fried Liver in Orange and Brandy Sauce

Serves 4
Working (and total) time: about 15 minutes

Calories **340**	350 g	pig's liver, thinly sliced	12 oz
Protein **29g**	2 tbsp	safflower oil	2 tbsp
Cholesterol **235mg**	2	onions, sliced	2
Total fat **18g**	1	sweet green pepper, seeded, deribbed and sliced	1
Saturated fat **5g**	1	garlic clove, chopped	1
Sodium **290mg**	1 tbsp	plain flour	1 tbsp
	2 tbsp	tomato paste	2 tbsp
	3	oranges, two peeled, halved and sliced, juice only of the third	3
	12.5 cl	unsalted vegetable stock (recipe, page 139)	4 fl oz
	½ tsp	salt	½ tsp
		freshly ground black pepper	
	2 tbsp	brandy	2 tbsp
	3 tbsp	single cream (optional)	3 tbsp

Heat the oil in a wok or large heavy frying pan over high heat and cook the liver until it has coloured — 3 to 4 minutes. Remove the liver from the pan and set it aside while you make the sauce.

Add the sliced onions, green pepper and garlic to the pan and cook over low heat for 5 to 10 minutes to soften them. Stir in the flour and tomato paste, then gradually add the orange juice and vegetable stock. Season with the salt and some freshly ground pepper and bring to the boil, stirring continuously.

Reserve a few orange slices for a garnish; add the remaining slices of orange to the pan with the cooked liver and the brandy, and heat through for another minute. Remove the pan from the heat and stir in the cream, if you are using it. Serve the liver garnished with the reserved orange slices.

SUGGESTED ACCOMPANIMENT: *plain boiled rice.*

Loire Escalopes

Serves 4
Working time: about 20 minutes
Total time: about 40 minutes

Calories **310**
Protein **19g**
Cholesterol **75mg**
Total fat **9g**
Saturated fat **4g**
Sodium **290mg**

4	pork escalopes (about 100g/3½ oz each), trimmed of fat	4
½ tsp	salt	½ tsp
	freshly ground black pepper	
8	shallots	8
¼ litre	Sancerre, Sauvignon or other Loire wine	8 fl oz
4	black peppercorns	4
1	fresh tarragon sprig	1
½ tsp	unsalted butter	½ tsp
1 tsp	sugar	1 tsp
1 tsp	grapeseed or olive oil	1 tsp
60 g	black seedless grapes, or other black grapes, halved and seeded	2 oz
60 g	green seedless grapes, or other green grapes, halved and seeded	2 oz
½ tsp	arrowroot	½ tsp
8 cl	unsweetened grape juice or unsalted veal stock (recipe, page 139)	3 fl oz
1 tbsp	finely chopped fresh tarragon	1 tbsp
1 tbsp	finely chopped fresh chervil	1 tbsp
1 tbsp	finely chopped lemon verbena or lemon balm	1 tbsp

Beat the escalopes lightly to tenderize them *(page 12, above, Step 2)*, season with the salt and some pepper, and set aside.

In a heavy-bottomed saucepan, simmer the shallots in half the wine with the peppercorns and tarragon, until softened — about 20 minutes — then add the butter and sugar, and toss over a fairly high heat until all the liquid has evaporated and the shallots are lightly caramelized. Remove the shallots from the pan and reserve them. Discard the tarragon; deglaze the pan with a little more wine and set aside.

Heat the oil in a heavy or non-stick frying pan. Brown the escalopes and cook them for about 2 minutes on each side; ensure that the meat is cooked through but do not overcook. Remove the escalopes from the pan and keep them warm.

Deglaze the frying pan with a spoonful or two of the remaining wine; add the wine used to deglaze the shallot saucepan, and allow to reduce for a moment; finally, add the rest of the wine, with the grapes and shallots, and warm through. Dissolve the arrowroot in 1 tablespoon of the grape juice or stock, stir this into the rest of the grape juice or stock and add to the wine and grapes. Bring to the boil, stirring constantly, and simmer until the sauce is slightly thickened and clear — about 1 minute. Return the escalopes to the pan to warm through, then stir in the tarragon, chervil and lemon verbena, and serve immediately.

Caper Escalopes

Serves 4
Working (and total) time: about 20 minutes

Calories **190**
Protein **20g**
Cholesterol **60mg**
Total fat **10g**
Saturated fat **4g**
Sodium **260mg**

4	pork escalopes (about 100g/3½ oz each), trimmed of fat	4
½ tsp	salt	½ tsp
	freshly ground black pepper	
	cayenne pepper (optional)	
2 tsp	dry mustard powder	2 tsp
1 tsp	safflower oil	1 tsp
2 tbsp	Marsala	2 tbsp
1	orange, grated rind of half, juice of whole	1
1 tbsp	capers, rinsed, drained and chopped	1 tbsp
1 tsp	green peppercorns, rinsed and drained	1 tsp
1 tsp	ground cinnamon	1 tsp
45 g	crème fraîche	1½ oz
125 g	fromage frais	4 oz

Beat the escalopes lightly to tenderize them *(page 12, above, Step 2)*, season with the salt and a little black pepper and, if you are using it, a pinch of cayenne; then dust them with the mustard powder.

Brush a heavy or non-stick frying pan with the oil. Brown the escalopes briefly and cook them for 2 minutes on each side; ensure that the meat is cooked through but do not overcook. Remove the escalopes from the pan and keep them warm.

Deglaze the frying pan with the Marsala over high heat until almost evaporated. Add the orange juice and rind and reduce until syrupy in appearance. Stir in the capers, peppercorns, cinnamon and *crème fraîche*, bring to the boil and reduce again very briefly. Remove the pan from the heat and stir in the *fromage frais*. Return the sauce briefly to the heat to amalgamate the flavours, then serve immediately with the escalopes.

SUGGESTED ACCOMPANIMENT: *parslied potatoes.*

Fillet with Mushrooms and Water Chestnuts

Calories **275**
Protein **24g**
Cholesterol **70mg**
Total fat **10g**
Saturated fat **4g**
Sodium **290mg**

Serves 4
Working time: about 30 minutes
Total time: about 1 hour and 30 minutes (includes chilling)

500 g	pork fillet, trimmed of fat	1 lb
100 g	water chestnuts, fresh or canned	3½ oz
¼ litre	unsalted vegetable stock (recipe, page 139) reduced to 15 cl (¼ pint)	8 fl oz
200 g	button mushrooms, finely sliced	7 oz
4 tbsp	dry white wine	4 tbsp
1 tsp	fresh lemon juice	1 tsp
5 cm	piece fresh ginger root	2 inch
1 tbsp	safflower oil	1 tbsp
2	garlic cloves, crushed	2
½ tsp	salt	½ tsp
	freshly ground black pepper	
45 g	crème fraîche	1½ oz
90 g	fromage frais	3 oz
	finely chopped fresh chives or spring onions, for garnish (optional)	

Chill the pork in the freezer for 1 hour to make it easier to cut, then slice it into rounds as thinly as possible.

If you are using fresh water chestnuts, scrub and peel them; canned chestnuts will be ready peeled. Slice the chestnuts into rounds as finely as possible.

In a saucepan, simmer the water chestnut slices in the reduced stock for 10 minutes, to allow them to absorb its flavour. Cook the mushrooms in the wine and lemon juice for 2 minutes in another saucepan. Drain the chestnuts and mushrooms and set them aside, reserving their cooking liquids.

Cut the ginger root into four or five pieces and use a garlic press to squeeze the juice, or grate the ginger root and pass it through a fine sieve. In a frying pan, heat a little of the oil with one of the garlic cloves and about one third of the ginger juice over gentle heat for a minute or two, then discard the garlic and increase the heat to medium high.

Season the meat with the salt and a little pepper, and quickly arrange about half of the slices in the frying pan. When the upper surface of each slice is nearly transparent — 30 to 45 seconds — turn and brown the other side. Lift the slices of pork out of the frying pan and keep them warm. Heat the rest of the safflower oil with the remaining garlic clove and one third of the ginger juice as before, and brown the remaining slices of pork.

Once all the meat is cooked, gently wipe excess fat from the frying pan, but retain any brown sediment and deglaze the pan quickly with the wine used to cook the mushrooms. When this has all but boiled away, add the stock used to cook the water chestnuts and reduce it quickly until it is slightly syrupy in appearance. Add the *crème fraîche* to the pan and reduce the sauce for a few seconds.

Strain the sauce through a fine-meshed sieve and wipe out the pan. Return the sauce to the pan, along with the meat, water chestnuts and mushrooms. Heat the pan gently to warm through all the ingredients, then stir in the *fromage frais*, and continue to heat for another 30 seconds — do not allow to bubble too hard, however, as this would cause the sauce to separate. Finally, stir in the remaining ginger juice and serve the dish immediately, without further heating, lightly sprinkled with the chives or spring onions if you are using them.

SUGGESTED ACCOMPANIMENTS: *plain brown rice; mange-tout.*

Pork Saltimbocca

ALTHOUGH TRADITIONALLY MADE WITH THIN SLICES OF VEAL, THIS
ITALIAN DISH TASTES EQUALLY GOOD WHEN MADE WITH LEAN PORK.

Serves 4
Working (and total) time: about 20 minutes

Calories **200**
Protein **22g**
Cholesterol **70mg**
Total fat **10g**
Saturated fat **4g**
Sodium **210mg**

4	pork escalopes (about 100 g/3½ oz each), trimmed of fat	4
1 tbsp	strong grainy mustard	1 tbsp
2	slices prosciutto (about 20g/¾ oz each)	2
12	small leaves fresh sage	12
6	leaves fresh lovage, halved	6
1 tsp	unsalted butter	1 tsp
4 tbsp	Marsala	4 tbsp
	balsamic vinegar (optional)	
	freshly ground black pepper	

Beat the escalopes firmly with a mallet until they have
doubled in size *(page 12, above, Step 2)*. Spread the
mustard over one surface of each escalope. Place one
slice of prosciutto over the mustard on each of two escalopes; divide the sage and lovage leaves between
the other two and press them firmly into the mustard.

Press each prosciutto-covered escalope on to a
herb-covered escalope to make two sandwiches with
a prosciutto and herb filling. Using a very sharp knife,
cut each escalope sandwich crosswise into six pieces.

If you have a large enough frying pan, cook in a
single batch; otherwise cook in two batches, dividing
the butter accordingly. Melt the butter in a heavy frying
pan over fairly high heat, until sizzling. Quickly, but
carefully, place the escalope sandwiches in the pan
and cook for 45 seconds to 1 minute, until the centre is
no longer pink. Turn with a fish slice and cook the second side for a further 30 to 45 seconds, maintaining a
fairly high heat.

Pour the Marsala into the pan and allow to bubble
up quickly. When reduced by half — about 30
seconds — add a little balsamic vinegar, if you wish,
and some black pepper. Serve immediately, dividing
the saltimbocca equally among four plates.

SUGGESTED ACCOMPANIMENT: *crisp, colourful salad with
balsamic vinaigrette.*

EDITOR'S NOTE: *Either the sage or the lovage may be omitted,
in which case you should double the quantity of the herb you
are using. Watercress leaves, in more generous quantity, may
be substituted for both the herbs. Smaller saltimbocca can be
made using 500 g (1 lb) of trimmed pork fillet, cut into 16
slices and beaten out.*

Medallions of Pork with Two Green Purées

Serves 4
Working time: about 1 hour
Total time: about 7 hours (includes marinating)

Calories **290**
Protein **25g**
Cholesterol **70mg**
Total fat **18g**
Saturated fat **4g**
Sodium **185mg**

500 g	pork fillet, trimmed of fat	1 lb
2	large sweet green peppers, seeded and deribbed	2
2 tsp	green peppercorns, rinsed and drained if bottled	2 tsp
4 cm	piece fresh ginger root	1½ inch
2 tbsp	virgin olive oil	2 tbsp
1 tbsp	wine vinegar	1 tbsp
¼ tsp	salt	¼ tsp
500 g	fresh sharp gooseberries	1 lb
2	fresh mint sprigs	2
1 tbsp	fructose	1 tbsp
60 g	fresh sorrel	2 oz
150 g	fromage frais	5 oz

Using a sharp knife, slice the fillet into 20 thin rounds, then beat them out until they are about half as large again (*page 12, above*).

Combine the green peppers, peppercorns, two thirds of the ginger, half the oil, and the vinegar and salt in a food processor. Or chop the ginger root and green peppers, and pound the ingredients together in a mortar. Coat the meat with this marinade and leave to marinate in a non-reactive dish for about 6 hours at room temperature (or 12 hours in the refrigerator).

To prepare the two purées, first wash and cook the gooseberries in a little water with the mint and fructose, until they are soft. Drain the cooked gooseberries and pass them through a sieve or purée them in a food processor or blender; there is no need to top and tail the berries prior to sieving. If using a food processor or blender — which give a creamy texture to the purée — sieve the purée after processing.

Wash the sorrel and strip the leaves from the stems. Cook the leaves with a little additional water until they are broken down and almost puréed. Beat the sorrel into the *fromage frais* and, using a garlic press, squeeze the juice from the remaining piece of fresh ginger into the mixture (or grate the ginger finely, sieve it, and add to the mixture). Keep the two purées warm in bowls set in pans of simmering water.

Wipe the marinade ingredients off the pieces of meat, which should by now be pale and very tender. It does not matter if a little of the pepper mixture adheres to the meat — the very brief cooking time will not allow this to burn. Heat half of the remaining oil in a wide, heavy frying pan and cook half of the meat gently for up to 1 minute on each side; browning is not essential. Remove from the pan and keep warm while cooking the second batch in the remaining oil. Serve the medallions immediately, accompanied by the purées.

SUGGESTED ACCOMPANIMENT: *mange-tout or green salad.*

EDITOR'S NOTE: *If you need to reheat the purées when the meat is ready to serve, the addition of a little arrowroot will prevent the sorrel-fromage frais mixture from separating. Fructose, or fruit sugar, is a very sweet natural sugar occurring in honey and many fruits.*

Home-Made Pork Sausages

SHOP-BOUGHT SAUSAGES CONTAIN A HIGH PROPORTION OF
FAT. IN THESE TWO VERSIONS OF ONE RECIPE, THE PROPORTION
OF FAT TO LEAN MEAT IS NO MORE THAN 1:6 AFTER TRIMMING.

Serves 10 (makes about 20 sausages)
Working time: about 1 hour
Total time: about 2 hours

Calories **300**
Protein **14g**
Cholesterol **60mg**
Total fat **24g**
Saturated fat **9g**
Sodium **280mg**

1 kg	neck end of pork, trimmed of excess fat	2 lb
3 to 3½ metres	natural lamb sausage casings, soaked in acidulated water for about 1 hour	9 to 10 feet
Seasonings for "Irish" sausages		
350 g	cooked potato, mashed or diced	12 oz
2 tbsp	whiskey	2 tbsp
1 tsp	white pepper	1 tsp
2 tsp	salt	2 tsp
1 tsp	yellow mustard seeds	1 tsp
1 tsp	ground caraway seeds	1 tsp
2 tsp	finely chopped fresh thyme	2 tsp
1 tsp	finely chopped fresh sage	1 tsp
Seasonings for "French" sausages		
250 g	lightly poached dessert apple, chopped	8 oz
1 tbsp	calvados or cognac	1 tbsp
1 tsp	quatre épices	1 tsp
4 tsp	finely chopped fresh basil	4 tsp
2 tsp	finely chopped fresh marjoram	2 tsp
1 tsp	finely chopped fresh mint	1 tsp
2 tsp	salt	2 tsp

Dice the meat and pass it through the medium blade
of a mincer, or chop it finely in a food processor. Mix
the meat with all the Irish or all the French seasoning
ingredients, according to which type of sausage you
are making, and again pass it through the mincer or
processor. Cook a teaspoon of the mixture in a dry
non-stick pan for 2 to 3 minutes, then taste and adjust
the herb and spice seasonings, as required.

Cut the casings into lengths of about 1 metre (3
feet). Roll one end of a length over the spout of a funnel or tap and run cold water through it to open it out
and check for punctures (Step 1, opposite). Rinse the
other casings in the same way and drain them. Roll
one casing over the nozzle of the sausage-making
attachment on the mincer or on to the equivalent on a
food processor; leave about 10 cm (4 inches) of casing
hanging free and tie a knot in the end.

Put the sausage mixture in the mincer and fill the
casing as described in Step 2, opposite; if you are
using a processor, follow the manufacturer's instructions. Fill the remaining casings in the same way, then
twist the casings at intervals of about 15 cm (6 inches)
to form individual sausages (Step 3, opposite).

Before cooking, separate the sausage links and
moisten the casings, but do not pierce them. Place the
sausages in a non-stick frying pan and add cold water
to cover the base. Bring to the boil and brown the
sausages by allowing the water to evaporate, then
reduce the heat and cook gently for 15 to 20 minutes,
turning them either with a spatula or by shaking the
pan; add more water if necessary to prevent sticking.

EDITOR'S NOTE: *Instead of sautéing, the sausages may be
baked in a 190°C (375°F or Mark 5) oven for 30 to 40 minutes.*

Making Sausages

1 RINSING THE CASINGS. After soaking the casings, cut them into lengths of about 1 metre (3 feet). Roll one end of each casing on to the spout of a funnel or tap and run cold water through it (above); discard any casings that are punctured. Lay out the casings to drain.

2 FILLING A CASING. Secure a sausage-making attachment to the mincer. Roll a casing on to its nozzle; leave about 10 cm (4 inches) loose and tie a knot in the end. Fill the mincer's bowl with the stuffing and turn the handle. As the casing fills, gradually slip it off the nozzle (above).

3 FORMING LINKS. When only about 10 cm (4 inches) of the casing remains to be filled, slip it off the nozzle and knot it. Roll the casing on a work surface to even out the stuffing. To form links, twist the casing through three or four turns at intervals of about 15 cm (6 inches), as shown above.

Noisettes in a Sherry Vinegar Sauce

Serves 4
Working (and total) time: about 20 minutes

Calories **270**
Protein **24g**
Cholesterol **70mg**
Total fat **14g**
Saturated fat **5g**
Sodium **320mg**

500 g	pork fillet, trimmed of fat and cut into 16 slices	1 lb
	freshly ground black pepper	
1 tbsp	virgin olive oil	1 tbsp
10	garlic cloves, peeled	10
3 tbsp	sherry or red wine vinegar	3 tbsp
1 tbsp	dry sherry	1 tbsp
2 tbsp	unsalted chicken or veal stock (recipes, page 139)	2 tbsp
750 g	ripe tomatoes, skinned, seeded and chopped, or 400 g (14 oz) canned whole tomatoes, drained	1½ lb
15 g	unsalted butter (optional)	½ oz
¼ tsp	salt	¼ tsp
30 g	finely chopped parsley or chives	1 oz

Season the pork generously with pepper, pressing it in with your fingers. Heat the oil in a heavy frying pan over high heat and, when it is smoking, add the pork. Brown the pork quickly on both sides and reduce the heat to very low. Add the garlic. Continue cooking until the pork is firm but still springy when you press it with a finger — 5 to 8 minutes, depending on thickness. Remove the pork from the pan and keep it warm.

Increase the heat and deglaze the pan with the vinegar. When it has all but disappeared, add the sherry and reduce for about 1 minute. Add the stock and tomatoes, and cook over high heat until reduced by half. Remove from the heat and pass the mixture through a sieve. Lower the heat, return the sauce and the meat to the pan and reheat briefly; if you wish, add the butter, off the heat, to thicken the sauce.

Season the pork with the salt, arrange it on four plates and spoon the sauce round it. Garnish with the chopped parsley or chives before serving.

SUGGESTED ACCOMPANIMENT: French beans.

Patties with Aubergine Purée

Serves 4
Working (and total) time: about 30 minutes

Calories **220**
Protein **23g**
Cholesterol **70mg**
Total fat **12g**
Saturated fat **4g**
Sodium **120mg**

450 g	trimmed leg or neck end of pork, minced	15 oz
20 g	spring onion, white part only, finely chopped	¾ oz
2 tsp	ground coriander	2 tsp
500 g	aubergines	1 lb
1¼ tsp	cumin seeds	1¼ tsp
1	shallot, finely chopped	1
45 g	fromage frais	1½ oz
	freshly ground black pepper	
1 tbsp	safflower oil	1 tbsp
	fresh coriander sprigs, for garnish	

Mix the minced pork with the finely chopped spring onions and ground coriander, and form it into eight patties measuring about 6 cm (2½ inches) in diameter.

Cut the aubergines in half lengthwise and place them in a vegetable steamer. Lay a sheet of grease-proof paper over the top, and steam until they are tender — about 10 minutes.

Heat the cumin seeds in a non-stick frying pan over medium heat, stirring frequently, for about 3 minutes. Add the finely chopped shallot and cook it until it has softened. Scoop the flesh from the aubergine halves and purée it in a food processor or a blender together with the contents of the frying pan. Return the mixture to the pan, and stir in the *fromage frais* and some freshly ground black pepper.

Heat the oil in another non-stick frying pan, over high heat, and brown the pork patties for 2 minutes on each side, then reduce the heat and cook for a further 3 minutes. Meanwhile, gently warm the purée over low heat, stirring constantly.

Spoon the purée on to four warmed plates. Place two pork patties on each plate and garnish with the sprigs of coriander.

Porkburgers

Serves 4
Working (and total) time: about 35 minutes

Calories **340**
Protein **32g**
Cholesterol **85mg**
Total fat **12g**
Saturated fat **4g**
Sodium **550 mg**

250 g	pork fillet, trimmed of fat and minced	8 oz
250 g	topside of veal, trimmed of fat and minced	8 oz
1	onion, very finely chopped	1
¼ tsp	salt	¼ tsp
½ tsp	dry mustard	½ tsp
¼ tsp	chili powder	¼ tsp
1 tbsp	safflower oil	1 tbsp
4	wholemeal baps, split in half	4
4	crisp lettuce leaves, washed and dried	4
4	slices beef tomato	4
4	mild or hot pickled chili peppers	4
Chili topping		
4 tbsp	chili relish	4 tbsp
1	carrot, grated	1
2	shallots, finely chopped	2
2.5 cm	piece cucumber, finely chopped	1 inch

In a bowl, mix the pork with the veal, onion, salt, dry mustard and chili powder. Form the mixture into four burger shapes about 1 cm (½ inch) thick.

Heat the oil in a large heavy frying pan over medium heat. Add the porkburgers and cook them for 5 to 6 minutes on each side.

Meanwhile, make the topping. In a bowl, mix the chili relish with the carrot, shallots and cucumber. Warm the baps under a medium-hot grill.

Arrange a lettuce leaf on the base portion of each bap, then add a porkburger to each, and top with a slice of tomato and a spoonful of chili topping. Cover with the bap lids and secure them in position with cocktail sticks. Garnish the burgers with the pickled chili peppers, and serve at once.

greaseproof paper and keep it warm.

Heat the oil in a heavy frying pan over low heat and cook the patties, turning them and gradually increasing the heat so that they become crisp and brown all over. This should take about 7 minutes. Remove the patties from the pan and keep them warm.

Over high heat, deglaze the pan with the balsamic vinegar. When it has all but disappeared, add 4 tablespoons of the reserved cooking liquid and reduce until it becomes syrupy. Add the remaining nutmeg and season lightly with the salt and some pepper.

Serve the patties on warmed plates with the sauce poured round them and the wild rice to one side.

EDITOR'S NOTE: *To make a richer and more glossy sauce, add reduced chicken stock instead of the rice-cooking liquid to the deglazed frying pan.*

Watercress Pork

Serves 4
Working (and total) time: about 25 minutes

Calories **195**
Protein **25g**
Cholesterol **70mg**
Total fat **10g**
Saturated fat **5g**
Sodium **275mg**

450 g	pork fillet, trimmed of fat and cut into 7.5 by 1.5 cm (3 by ¾ inch) strips	15 oz
125 g	watercress, leaves and fine stems	4 oz
30 cl	unsalted veal stock (recipe, page 139)	½ pint
1	shallot, finely chopped	1
3 tbsp	dry white wine	3 tbsp
75 g	fromage frais	2½ oz
¼ tsp	salt	¼ tsp
	freshly ground black pepper	

Reserve some of the watercress for garnish; bring the stock to the boil and blanch the remaining watercress for 1 minute. Drain, reserving the stock, then refresh the watercress under cold running water. Drain the watercress again, then place it on paper towels to dry.

Heat a non-stick frying pan, add the pork and cook briskly for 2 to 3 minutes, turning the strips so they become an even light brown on the outside and are only lightly cooked in the centre. Transfer the strips to a warmed plate using a slotted spoon, and cover to keep warm. Reduce the heat beneath the pan, add the shallot and wine, and cook, stirring occasionally, until the shallots have softened and the wine has almost completely evaporated — 3 to 4 minutes. Add the reserved stock, increase the heat and reduce the liquid until there are only about 3 tablespoons left; add any juices from the meat dish towards the end of the reduction. In a food processor or blender, purée the watercress with the reduced stock. Add the *fromage frais* and purée again. Season with the salt and some pepper.

In a saucepan, reheat the sauce over low heat, stirring; just before serving, add the pork and fold through gently to coat the strips. Serve garnished with the reserved watercress.

SUGGESTED ACCOMPANIMENT: *couscous or noodles.*

Prune and Pecan Patties

Serves 4
Working time: about 20 minutes
Total time: about 1 hour and 30 minutes

Calories **280**
Protein **16g**
Cholesterol **45mg**
Total fat **12g**
Saturated fat **4g**
Sodium **150mg**

250 g	pork fillet, minced	8 oz
30 cl	unsalted chicken stock (recipe, page 139) or water	½ pint
90 g	wild rice	3 oz
8	prunes, stoned and soaked in 1 tbsp of dry Madeira for 1 hour	8
50 g	pecan nuts	1¾ oz
1½ tsp	grated nutmeg	1½ tsp
1 tbsp	arachide or sunflower oil	1 tbsp
3 tbsp	balsamic vinegar	3 tbsp
¼ tsp	salt	¼ tsp
	freshly ground black pepper	

In a saucepan, bring the stock or water to the boil and add the wild rice. Cook the rice, covered, for about 1 hour, checking it periodically and adding more stock or water if necessary. Meanwhile, chop the prunes and pecan nuts finely and combine them with the minced pork and ½ teaspoon of the nutmeg. Shape the mixture into eight patties with your hands.

When the rice is cooked — the grain should be split open and soft, but still have some bite — drain it and reserve the cooking liquid. Cover the rice with wet

Pepper Pork with Mozzarella

Serves 4
Working time: about 25 minutes
Total time: about 40 minutes

Calories **240**
Protein **25g**
Cholesterol **90mg**
Total fat **14g**
Saturated fat **5g**
Sodium **225mg**

500 g	pork fillet, trimmed of fat	1 lb
1 tsp	green peppercorns	1 tsp
1 tsp	black peppercorns	1 tsp
1 tbsp	safflower oil	1 tbsp
1	garlic clove, halved	1
60 g	low-fat mozzarella, grated	2 oz
2	shallots, finely chopped	2
	Tabasco sauce	
	Worcester sauce	
15 cl	unsalted chicken stock (recipe, page 139)	¼ pint
2 tbsp	dry sherry	2 tbsp
4	flat-leaf parsley sprigs	4

Lay the pork fillet on a board and, with a sharp knife, cut it at a slightly diagonal angle into 12 slices, each about 2 cm (¾ inch) wide. Crush the green and black peppercorns using a pestle and mortar. Sprinkle the pepper over one side of the pork slices and press it into the meat. Cover, and set aside for 15 minutes.

Heat the oil in a large frying pan over medium heat. Add the garlic and the pork slices, peppered side down, and cook over medium heat for 3 to 4 minutes on each side, until well browned. Preheat the grill. Remove the pork from the pan and arrange the slices, peppered side up, in two slightly overlapping rows in a shallow fireproof serving dish. Sprinkle the pork with the mozzarella and cook under the grill until the cheese has melted and is beginning to brown.

Meanwhile, discard the garlic from the frying pan. Add the shallots to the pan and stir well, scraping up any sediment from the bottom of the pan. Stir in a few drops each of Tabasco sauce and Worcester sauce, and add the stock and sherry. Simmer the sauce for about 3 minutes, until slightly reduced. Spoon the sauce round the pork steaks and serve at once, garnished with the parsley sprigs.

SUGGESTED ACCOMPANIMENTS: *tiny new potatoes; watercress, curly endive and green pepper salad.*

Escalopes with Tomato and Mozzarella

Serves 4
Working time: about 20 minutes
Total time: about 40 minutes

Calories **295**	4	pork escalopes (about 100 g/3½ oz each), trimmed of fat	4
Protein **25g**	2 tbsp	virgin olive oil	2 tbsp
Cholesterol **70mg**	1	small onion, finely chopped	1
Total fat **18g**	1	small carrot, finely chopped	1
Saturated fat **6g**	½	stick celery, finely chopped	½
Sodium **290mg**	750 g	ripe tomatoes, skinned and seeded, or 400 g (14 oz) canned tomatoes, drained	1½ lb
	1 tbsp	tomato paste	1 tbsp
	2	bay leaves	2
		freshly ground black pepper	
	45 g	fresh basil, chopped	1½ oz
	75 g	low-fat mozzarella, thinly sliced	2½ oz

Heat 1 tablespoon of the oil in a heavy-bottomed or non-stick saucepan and gently cook the chopped onion, carrot and celery until softened — about 3 minutes. Add the tomatoes, tomato paste and the bay leaves to the pan and cook for about 20 minutes, or until the sauce is no longer runny, stirring frequently.

Preheat the grill to high. Season the escalopes with some freshly ground pepper, rubbing it in with your fingertips. In a heavy or non-stick frying pan, heat the remaining oil over high heat until it is smoking, and brown the escalopes on both sides for 1 minute. Remove the pan from the heat and allow the meat to sizzle for a couple of minutes, turning once.

Transfer the escalopes to a grill rack and spread over them equal portions of the tomato sauce, then sprinkle with the basil and top with the mozzarella. Heat under the hot grill for 1 minute or until the cheese has melted. Serve immediately.

SUGGESTED ACCOMPANIMENT: *plain boiled rice and green salad.*

Pork with a Passion Fruit Sauce

Serves 4
Working time: about 15 minutes
Total time: about 3 hours and 15 minutes
(includes marinating)

Calories **260**
Protein **32g**
Cholesterol **70mg**
Total fat **11g**
Saturated fat **4g**
Sodium **110mg**

4	pork loin steaks (about 125 g/4 oz each), trimmed of fat	4
4	passion fruit	4
17.5 cl	dry white wine	6 fl oz
	white pepper	
1 tsp	sugar (optional)	1 tsp

Beat the steaks with a mallet to flatten them slightly (page 12, above, Step 2), then place them in a single layer in a shallow non-reactive dish.

Squeeze the juice from the passion fruit; reserve the seeds. Pour the juice on to the pork and spread the seeds over the surface. Cover the dish and leave in a cool place for 3 hours, turning the pork frequently.

Preheat the grill to very high. Remove the pork from the marinade and brush off any seeds adhering to it; reserve the marinade. Place the steaks close to the source of heat and grill for about 4 minutes on each side, until lightly charred on the surface but still tender in the centre.

Meanwhile, in a small pan, boil the wine until it is reduced to about 4 tablespoons, then stir in the reserved marinade and heat through. Taste the sauce and add the sugar if desired; season with some white pepper. Serve the pork with the sauce spooned over.

EDITOR'S NOTE: If preferred, the passion fruit juice may be strained and the seeds discarded.

Chili Peppers — a Cautionary Note

Both dried and fresh hot chili peppers should be handled with care. Their flesh and seeds contain volatile oils that can make skin tingle and cause eyes to burn. Rubber gloves offer protection — but the cook should still be careful not to touch the face, lips or eyes when working with chili peppers.

Soaking fresh chili peppers in cold, salted water for an hour will remove some of their fire. If canned chilies are substituted for fresh ones, they should be rinsed in cold water in order to eliminate as much of the brine used to preserve them as possible.

Indian Chops

Serves 4
Working time: about 25 minutes
Total time: about 1 day (includes marinating)

Calories **290**		
Protein **40g**		
Cholesterol **70mg**		
Total fat **14g**		
Saturated fat **5g**		
Sodium **225mg**		

4	pork chops (about 175 g/6 oz each), trimmed of fat	4
1	fresh chili pepper, or dried chili pepper soaked in water for 30 minutes, seeded and chopped (caution, box, opposite)	1
2	garlic cloves	2
1	small piece turmeric	1
½ tsp	fenugreek seeds	½ tsp
½ tsp	coriander seeds	½ tsp
½ tsp	cumin seeds	½ tsp
½ tsp	salt	½ tsp
4 tbsp	plain low-fat yogurt	4 tbsp

Using a mortar and pestle, pound the chili pepper with the garlic, turmeric and other seasonings into a coarse paste. Mix the yogurt into the paste and blend well.

Coat the pork chops with the yogurt mixture, place them in a non-reactive dish, cover with plastic film and leave to marinate in the refrigerator for 24 hours.

Preheat the grill to very hot. Remove the chops from the marinade, wipe them with paper towels and brush off any dry ingredients that are sticking to them. Heat two metal skewers over high heat on the stove and print a criss-cross pattern on both sides of each chop by pressing the skewer gently on to the surface.

Cook the chops for 7 minutes on each side, or until cooked through. Leave the chops in a warm place to rest for 5 minutes before serving.

SUGGESTED ACCOMPANIMENTS: *new potatoes tossed in toasted poppy seeds; cucumber in yogurt and mint dressing.*

EDITOR'S NOTE: *Ground spices may be substituted for the turmeric stem and the fenugreek, coriander and cumin seeds, but grinding the ingredients in a mortar yields a better flavour. About ½ teaspoon of mustard powder may be used instead of the chili peppers. If you barbecue the chops on a grid over charcoal, you do not need to sear them with a skewer.*

Pork Chops with Kumquats

Serves 4
Working time: about 20 minutes
Total time: about 2 hours and 20 minutes
(includes marinating)

Calories **320**		
Protein **33g**		
Cholesterol **80mg**		
Total fat **13g**		
Saturated fat **6g**		
Sodium **280mg**		

4	pork chops (125 to 150 g/ 4½ to 5 oz each), trimmed of fat	4
6 tbsp	dry white wine or vermouth	6 tbsp
6 tbsp	fresh orange juice	6 tbsp
2 tsp	clear honey	2 tsp
250 g	ripe kumquats	8 oz
½ tsp	salt	½ tsp
	freshly ground black pepper	
15 g	unsalted butter, chilled	½ oz

Combine the wine or vermouth with the orange juice and honey in a non-reactive dish. Add the pork and leave to marinate for at least 2 hours.

Remove the meat from the dish and reserve the marinade. Pat the meat dry with paper towels and set it aside. Preheat the grill.

Reserve four kumquats for garnish; purée the rest in a food processor with the reserved marinade, then pass it through a fine sieve. In a small pan over high heat, reduce the purée for about 1 minute or until thick and bright orange. Remove from the heat.

Season the pork with the salt and a little pepper and cook under the hot grill for 5 minutes on each side, or until cooked through. Reheat the sauce then, off the heat, whisk in the chilled butter to thicken it. Serve the chops with the sauce spooned round them, garnished with thin slices of the reserved kumquats.

Chops with Mustard and Dill Sauce

Serves 6
Working (and total) time: about 25 minutes

Calories **260**		
Protein **34g**		
Cholesterol **80mg**		
Total fat **17g**		
Saturated fat **7g**		
Sodium **350mg**		

6	pork chops (125 to 150 g/ 4½ to 5 oz each), trimmed of fat	6
3 tbsp	red peppercorns	3 tbsp
250 g	thick Greek yogurt	8 oz
1 tbsp	prepared English mustard	1 tbsp
1½ tbsp	chopped dill	1½ tbsp
½ tsp	salt	½ tsp

Preheat the grill to high. Crush the peppercorns in a mortar and press them on to both sides of the chops. Mix together the yogurt, mustard and dill, and season with salt. Refrigerate while you cook the chops.

Grill the chops for 7 to 8 minutes on each side, until the juices run clear when pricked with a skewer. Serve the chops immediately with the mustard and dill sauce.

EDITOR'S NOTE: *If red peppercorns are not available, crush a few juniper berries with some black peppercorns.*

Kebabs with Red Peppers and Grapefruit

Serves 6
Working time: about 20 minutes
Total time: about 1 hour and 15 minutes (includes marinating)

Calories **225**
Protein **22g**
Cholesterol **70mg**
Total fat **12g**
Saturated fat **3g**
Sodium **145mg**

750 g	pork fillet, trimmed of fat and cut into about 36 cubes	1½ lb
4 tbsp	safflower oil	4 tbsp
1 tbsp	wine vinegar	1 tbsp
2 tbsp	chopped chives	2 tbsp
¼ tsp	salt	¼ tsp
	freshly ground black pepper	
3	grapefruits	3
2 or 3	sweet red peppers	2 or 3

Mix together the oil, vinegar and chives, add the salt and a little pepper, and marinate the meat in this mix-ture for about 1 hour. While the meat marinates, slice off all the peel and pith from the grapefruits and divide them into segments; seed and derib the peppers and cut into 2.5 cm (1 inch) squares.

Remove the meat from the marinade and thread the cubes on to 12 small skewers, alternating one pepper square and one grapefruit segment between each cube. Preheat the grill to high and cook the kebabs for about 10 minutes, turning once — take care when turning not to break the grapefruit segments. The meat should be moist and the peppers still firm. Serve the kebabs immediately.

SUGGESTED ACCOMPANIMENTS: *plain boiled rice; green salad.*

EDITOR'S NOTE: *If you use wooden skewers, soak them in water for about 10 minutes before threading them with the pork — this will prevent them from burning under the grill.*

Kebabs in Tea and Ginger Marinade

Serves 4
Working time: about 35 minutes
Total time: about 9 hours (includes marinating)

Calories **160**
Protein **22g**
Cholesterol **70mg**
Total fat **8g**
Saturated fat **3g**
Sodium **80mg**

500 g	pork fillet, trimmed of fat and cut into 24 cubes	1 lb
16	shallots, peeled, or spring onion bulbs	16
16	button mushrooms	16

Tea marinade

1 tsp	Earl Grey tea leaves	1 tsp
1	garlic clove, crushed	1
2 tbsp	finely chopped fresh ginger root	2 tbsp
4 tbsp	dry sherry	4 tbsp
1 tbsp	light brown sugar	1 tbsp
2 tbsp	virgin olive oil	2 tbsp

To make the marinade, put the tea leaves in a jug and pour 12.5 cl (4 fl oz) of boiling water over the leaves. Leave to steep for 4 minutes, then strain into a bowl. Add the remaining marinade ingredients to the bowl and stir to mix well.

Add the pork cubes to the bowl and turn to coat with the marinade. Cover the bowl and put it in the refrigerator for 8 hours, or overnight.

When ready to cook, preheat the grill. Drain the meat, reserving the marinade. Thread the pork cubes alternating with the shallots and mushrooms on to eight skewers. Brush all over with the marinade and grill, about 12.5 cm (5 inches) from the source of heat, for 15 minutes, turning to cook evenly and basting frequently with the reserved marinade. Serve hot.

SUGGESTED ACCOMPANIMENT: *puréed swedes.*

EDITOR'S NOTE: If you use wooden skewers, soak them in water for about 10 minutes before threading them with the pork and vegetables to prevent them from burning under the grill.

Nordic Medallions

Serves 4
Working time: about 20 minutes
Total time: about 50 minutes (includes marinating)

Calories **220**
Protein **22g**
Cholesterol **70mg**
Total fat **12g**
Saturated fat **3g**
Sodium **280mg**

500 g	pork fillet, trimmed of fat	1 lb
12.5 cl	dry white wine	4 fl oz
1 tbsp	safflower oil	1 tbsp
3 tbsp	finely chopped dill	3 tbsp
1	large cucumber	1
½ tsp	salt	½ tsp
	freshly ground black pepper	
60 g	sweet-sour pickled cucumber (dill pickle)	2 oz
45 g	fromage frais	1½ oz

Slice the fillet diagonally into eight medallions, then beat out the medallions until they are about 5 mm (¼ inch) thick *(page 12, above)*. Lay the medallions in a non-reactive bowl with the wine, oil and 2 tablespoons of the dill. Leave to marinate for at least 30 minutes.

Towards the end of this time, peel the cucumber and cut it in half along its length. Using a teaspoon, scrape out the seeds and discard. Finely dice the flesh of the cucumber and tip it into a saucepan.

Remove the meat from the marinade and shake off excess liquid. Pour the marinade over the cucumber, add ¼ teaspoon of the salt and a little pepper, then bring to a lively boil. Cover and cook for 5 minutes, then remove the lid and, stirring all the time, reduce the liquid until the cucumber is quite dry. While the cucumber is cooking, finely dice the pickled cucumber and stir it into the pan with the remaining dill. Remove the pan from the heat. Preheat the grill.

Sprinkle the medallions with the remaining salt and some pepper, then sear them under the hot grill for 2 to 3 minutes on each side, until flecked with brown.

Quickly put the cucumber back on the heat, and stir in the *fromage frais* — do not allow the mixture to boil. Serve two medallions on each of four plates, with the cucumber spooned round them.

SUGGESTED ACCOMPANIMENT: *boiled new potatoes*.

Devilled Medallions

Serves 4
Working time: about 25 minutes
Total time: about 35 minutes

Calories **275**		
Protein **25g**		
Cholesterol **70mg**		
Total fat **8g**		
Saturated fat **3g**		
Sodium **320mg**		

500 g	boned pork loin, trimmed of fat and cut into eight medallions (about 1 cm/½ inch thick)	1 lb
2 tbsp	Dijon mustard	2 tbsp
3 tbsp	dry white wine	3 tbsp
½ tsp	hot paprika	½ tsp
	freshly ground black pepper	
175 g	fine dry brown breadcrumbs	6 oz
Peach chutney		
2	ripe peaches (about 250 g/8 oz)	2
1 tbsp	capers, chopped	1 tbsp
1 or 2	spring onions, finely chopped	1 or 2
1 tbsp	fresh lemon juice	1 tbsp

First make the chutney. Peel and stone both peaches, then purée one peach in a blender or food processor and pour into a bowl. Chop the other peach roughly and stir it into the purée with the capers, spring onions and lemon juice. Set aside.

Combine the mustard, wine, paprika and some black pepper in a shallow dish. Stir well until smooth. Spread out the breadcrumbs on a plate or a sheet of greaseproof paper. Dip the medallions, one at a time, in the mustard mixture and gently shake off excess, then coat both sides and round the edges with the crumbs, pressing them on with the blade of a table knife. Leave the coated medallions to dry briefly while you preheat the grill.

Grill the medallions under moderately high heat, about 12.5 cm (5 inches) from the heat source, for 5 minutes on each side, or until they are lightly browned and the pork is cooked through.

Arrange the medallions on a warm platter or individual plates. Serve with the chutney.

Pork Char-Shiu

CHAR-SHIU — IN CANTONESE, "ROASTED ON A FORK" — IS THE
NAME OF A CHINESE CHARCOAL-GRILLED PORK DISH. IN THIS
VERSION, ALL FAT IS TRIMMED OFF THE MEAT AND A LIGHT GLAZING
SYRUP KEEPS THE MEAT MOIST DURING COOKING; IT CAN BE
COOKED UNDER A GRILL OR, BETTER STILL, ON A BARBECUE.

Serves 4
Working time: about 30 minutes
Total time: about 3 hours and 30 minutes
(includes marinating)

Calories **230**
Protein **27g**
Cholesterol **90mg**
Total fat **9g**
Saturated fat **4g**
Sodium **100mg**

2	pork fillets (about 300 g/10 oz each), thin ends cut off, trimmed of fat	2
2 tbsp	low-sodium soy sauce or shoyu	2 tbsp
3 or 4	spring onions, finely chopped	3 or 4
2.5 cm	piece fresh ginger root, finely chopped	1 inch
2	garlic cloves, finely chopped	2
½ tsp	Sichuan pepper	½ tsp
2	star anise	2
1 tbsp	dry sherry	1 tbsp
1 tbsp	honey	1 tbsp
1½ tsp	red wine vinegar	1½ tsp
½ tsp	cornflour or potato flour, mixed with 2 tbsp water	½ tsp
	mixed salad leaves, washed and dried	

Rub the pork with 1 tablespoon of the soy sauce and
leave for 20 minutes in a cool place. In a mortar,
pound the spring onions, ginger and garlic to a rough
paste with the Sichuan pepper and star anise. Mix in
the sherry, the remaining soy sauce, half of the honey
and 1 teaspoon of the vinegar; coat the pork with the
paste and leave it to marinate for 2 to 6 hours in the
refrigerator, turning it once or twice.

Remove the pork from the refrigerator, pat it dry with
paper towels and discard any dry ingredients that are
sticking to it. Strain the marinade and reserve. Prepare
a glazing syrup by mixing 1 teaspoon of hot water with
the remaining honey and vinegar.

Preheat the grill to very hot, place the meat close to
the source of heat and brown it on both sides for 3 to 4
minutes. Move the meat to about 10 cm (4 inches) from

the heat source and continue to cook for a further 10 minutes, turning a few times and basting constantly with the glazing syrup. Test for doneness with a skewer — the juice that runs out should be almost clear. Cover the cooked fillet loosely with aluminium foil, and leave to rest for 5 minutes.

Heat the reserved marinade to a simmer, add the cornflour or potato flour mixture and bring back to simmer. To serve, cut the fillet across the grain into thin slices and place them on a bed of salad leaves. Serve the marinade separately as a dipping sauce.

SUGGESTED ACCOMPANIMENT: *plain boiled rice or stir-fried mixed vegetables.*

Pork Kofta

COMMON IN INDIAN AND MIDDLE-EASTERN COOKING, KOFTA CONSISTS OF MINCED MEAT AND SEASONINGS ROLLED INTO BALLS OR SAUSAGE SHAPES.

Serves 4
Working time: about 35 minutes
Total time: about 2 hours and 30 minutes
(includes marinating)

Calories **375**
Protein **30g**
Cholesterol **80mg**
Total fat **20g**
Saturated fat **5g**
Sodium **510mg**

500 g	minced pork fillet	1 lb
1	lemon, grated rind only	1
2	garlic cloves, crushed	2
1 tbsp	coriander seeds, toasted and coarsely ground	1 tbsp
½ tsp	salt	½ tsp
	freshly ground black pepper	
3 tbsp	dry white wine	3 tbsp
1½ tbsp	fresh lemon juice	1½ tbsp
1½ tbsp	virgin olive oil	1½ tbsp
4	carrots, grated	4
30 g	fresh coriander leaves, chopped	1 oz
4	pitta breads	4

Combine the pork with the lemon rind, garlic, coriander seeds, salt and some pepper. Divide into four and roll into sausage shapes about 15 by 2.5 cm (6 by 1 inch). Gently place the kofta in a shallow dish and pour on the wine, 1 tablespoon of the lemon juice and the oil. Leave to marinate for at least 2 hours, turning the kofta and coating with the marinade at frequent intervals.

Preheat the grill to high. Mix the carrots with the coriander leaves and the remaining lemon juice.

Remove the kofta from the marinade and grill them until the pork feels firm and is well browned on all sides — about 7 minutes. Meanwhile, warm the pitta bread through in a 170°C (325°F or Mark 3) oven.

When the kofta are cooked, carefully slit open one side of each pitta bread to make a pocket. Fill with a quarter of the carrot salad and one hot kofta.

SUGGESTED ACCOMPANIMENT: *yogurt, spooned into the pitta.*

Citrus Satay

Serves 4
Working (and total) time: about 45 minutes

Calories **220**
Protein **24g**
Cholesterol **85mg**
Total fat **12g**
Saturated fat **4g**
Sodium **400mg**

350 g	lean leg or neck end of pork, minced	12 oz
150 g	prawns, shelled and deveined	5 oz
1	garlic clove	1
1 cm	piece fresh ginger root	½ inch
½ tsp	fresh lime juice	½ tsp
½ tsp	arrowroot	½ tsp
¾ tsp	salt	¾ tsp
2 tbsp	chopped fresh coriander	2 tbsp
½ tsp	ground galangal	½ tsp
½ tsp	ground lemon grass	½ tsp
¼ tsp	ground dried lemon rind (optional)	¼ tsp
¼ tsp	tamarind concentrate (optional)	¼ tsp
2 tsp	safflower oil	2 tsp
Peanut-yogurt satay sauce		
45 g	shelled peanuts, toasted, skins removed	1½ oz
½ tsp	grated lime rind	½ tsp
1 tsp	fresh lime juice	1 tsp
½ tsp	dark brown sugar	½ tsp
1½ tsp	low-sodium soy sauce or shoyu	1½ tsp
⅛ tsp	salt	⅛ tsp
4 tbsp	plain low-fat yogurt	4 tbsp
⅛ tsp	chili powder	⅛ tsp

In a mortar, pound the prawns with the garlic, ginger, lime juice and arrowroot. Chill the prawn mixture to make it easier to handle.

Combine the pork with the salt, coriander, galangal and lemon grass, and the lemon rind and tamarind if using. Form the mixture into eight flat, oval patties. Spoon an eighth of the prawn mixture into the middle of each patty, then mould the pork round the filling to enclose it completely. Chill the patties if you are not cooking them immediately.

Preheat the grill. Insert a wooden satay stick or metal skewer through each patty; alternatively, the meat can be cooked and served without the sticks. Brush a grill pan lightly with a little of the oil, arrange the patties in the pan and brush their tops with a little more oil. Cook under medium heat, turning once, until golden-brown on both sides — about 10 minutes.

Meanwhile, make the sauce. Grind the nuts finely in a food processor, and add the lime rind and juice, sugar, soy sauce and salt. Beat in the yogurt and add the chili powder. Serve the sauce in a bowl.

SUGGESTED ACCOMPANIMENTS: *citrus rice; a crisp green salad or stir-fried vegetables.*

EDITOR'S NOTE: *The sauce may be prepared in advance but will thicken a little on standing. If using wooden skewers, soak them in water for about 10 minutes before threading them with the patties — to prevent them from burning.*

Mediterranean Kidneys

KIDNEYS ARE A RICH SOURCE OF VITAMINS BUT HAVE A RELATIVELY HIGH CHOLESTEROL CONTENT, WHICH SHOULD BE TAKEN INTO ACCOUNT WHEN PLANNING THE REST OF THE DAY'S MENU.

Serves 4
Working (and total) time: about 50 minutes

Calories **180**
Protein **8g**
Cholesterol **360mg**
Total fat **12g**
Saturated fat **5g**
Sodium **510mg**

4	pig's kidneys	4
1 tbsp	virgin olive oil	1 tbsp
1	garlic clove, finely chopped	1
250 g	bulb fennel, roughly chopped, feathery tops reserved for garnish	8 oz
250 g	ripe tomatoes, skinned, seeded and chopped	8 oz
1 tbsp	fresh lemon juice	1 tbsp
2 tbsp	chopped basil or oregano	2 tbsp
½ tsp	salt	½ tsp
	freshly ground black pepper	
30 g	unsalted butter, chilled	1 oz

Heat ½ tablespoon of the oil in a heavy-bottomed saucepan over low heat. Add the garlic, chopped fennel, tomatoes and lemon juice. Cover, and cook until the fennel is tender — about 30 minutes. Remove the lid and increase the heat; stirring all the time, boil off any liquid and cook the vegetables until just beginning to catch on the bottom of the pan. Stir in the basil or oregano, half of the salt and some black pepper.

Briefly purée the vegetables in a food processor or blender, or pass them through a sieve. Return the purée to the saucepan.

Peel off the fat and membrane from the kidneys and cut out the white cores (below). Preheat the grill to very hot. Thread two parallel thin short skewers through each kidney so that the kidneys will stay flat while

cooking. Brush all surfaces of the kidneys with the remaining oil and season with the remaining salt and some more black pepper.

Grill the kidneys for about 3 minutes on each side, so that the surfaces are well coloured but the insides are still pink. Remove the skewers; arrange the kidneys on a serving plate and keep them warm.

Cut the butter into tiny cubes, and beat them into the fennel purée over low heat until the sauce is glossy. Spoon the purée over the kidneys, garnish with the reserved fennel tops and serve immediately.

SUGGESTED ACCOMPANIMENT: *mixed salad with a mustard vinaigrette.*

EDITOR'S NOTE: *If you use wooden skewers, soak them in water for about 10 minutes before threading them with the kidneys — this will prevent them from burning under the grill.*

Preparing a Kidney

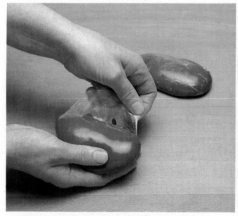

1 *PEELING OFF THE MEMBRANE. With a sharp knife, make a shallow slit in the rounded side of the kidney to pierce the translucent membrane that encloses it. Peel off the membrane and sever it from the core at the concave side of the kidney.*

2 *OPENING THE KIDNEY. Make a lengthwise cut into the kidney's rounded side until you feel the strands of core resisting the blade. Fold back the upper section then cut through the strands. Deepen the cut to within 5 mm (¼ inch) of the concave side.*

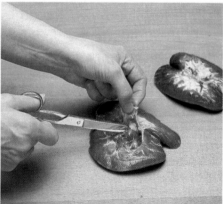

3 *CUTTING OUT THE CORE. With the kidney laid open on the work surface, use a pair of scissors to snip out the white core. Take care not to separate the two halves of the kidney.*

Prune Fillet Wrapped in Vine Leaves

Serves 6
Working time: about 30 minutes
Total time: about 5 hours (includes soaking)

Calories **280**
Protein **33g**
Cholesterol **70mg**
Total fat **11g**
Saturated fat **4g**
Sodium **100mg**

2	pork fillets (about 350 g/12 oz each), trimmed of fat	2
18	prunes, soaked for 4 hours in boiling water to cover plus 1 ½ tbsp brandy	18
½ tsp	salt	½ tsp
	freshly ground black pepper	
18	juniper berries	18
About 15	fresh vine leaves	About 15
5 tbsp	unsalted chicken stock (recipe, page 139)	5 tbsp

Remove the prunes from their soaking liquid when they are soft, and stone them; reserve the soaking liquid. Preheat the oven to 230°C (450°F or Mark 8).

Cut a lengthwise incision in each fillet and beat the fillets gently with a wooden mallet to flatten them *(page 11, below)*. Season the meat lightly with the salt and a little freshly ground pepper.

With the cut side of the fillets facing up, place the prunes and juniper berries down the centre of each fillet and fold the meat round them to make two long, thin rolls. Wrap the rolls with some of the vine leaves and tie them with string in several places. Put the wrapped rolls in a roasting tin with the stock, cover with foil and cook in the oven for 30 minutes.

Take the meat out of the oven and leave it to rest for 10 to 15 minutes. Add the reserved prune-soaking liquid to the juices in the tin and boil for 1 minute over medium heat, scraping up the deposits on the base of the tin with a spoon.

Arrange the remaining vine leaves on a warm serving dish. Slice the fillets and remove the string. Place the slices down the middle of the dish and pour the cooking juices over them.

EDITOR'S NOTE: *If you are using preserved vine leaves, rinse them first under cold running water to remove the salt. The vine leaves arranged on the serving dish will soak up some of the cooking juices and can be eaten.*

Broad Bean Pork

Serves 4
Working time: about 30 minutes
Total time: about 1 hour and 20 minutes

Calories **280**
Protein **33g**
Cholesterol **70mg**
Total fat **14g**
Saturated fat **4g**
Sodium **125mg**

500 g	boned pork loin, trimmed of fat	1 lb
	freshly ground black pepper	
125 g	cooked shelled young broad beans	4 oz
1 tbsp	thick Greek yogurt	1 tbsp
1 tsp	chopped fresh summer savory	1 tsp
1 tsp	fresh lemon juice	1 tsp
8 cl	dry white wine	3 fl oz
17.5 cl	unsalted veal stock (recipe, page 139)	6 fl oz

Preheat the oven to 180°C (350°F or Mark 4). Season the inside of the pork loin with a little freshly ground black pepper.

Purée the broad beans with the yogurt in a food processor, then pass the purée through a non-metallic sieve. Stir in the summer savory, add the lemon juice, and spread the mixture over the inside of the pork. Roll the pork up, lay a strip of foil over the exposed stuffing and tie it into shape with string.

Heat a heavy roasting tin or fireproof casserole, add the pork and cook over fairly high heat, turning the pork so that it browns evenly — about 5 minutes. Then transfer the casserole to the oven and cook until the pork is done — about 50 minutes.

Transfer the pork to a warmed plate, cover and leave to rest in a warm place. Stir the wine into the roasting tin and boil until almost completely evaporated. Stir in the stock and boil again until very slightly thickened. Taste, and add freshly ground black pepper and a little more lemon juice, if you wish. Carve the pork into slices, removing the foil and string, and spoon the sauce round each serving.

SUGGESTED ACCOMPANIMENT: *green noodles.*

EDITOR'S NOTE: *A boned loin of pork may also be stuffed with the spinach and mushroom mixture enclosed in a fillet in the recipe on page 52. For a 500 g (1 lb) loin, use half the amount of stuffing required for the fillet.*

Pot-Roast Loin with Cherry Tomatoes

Serves 6
Working time: about 20 minutes
Total time: about 1 hour and 20 minutes

Calories **260**
Protein **30g**
Cholesterol **70mg**
Total fat **13g**
Saturated fat **4g**
Sodium **90mg**

750 g	boned pork loin, trimmed of fat	1 ½ lb
1 tbsp	virgin olive oil	1 tbsp
2 tsp	fennel seeds	2 tsp
1 tsp	green peppercorns	1 tsp
2 tbsp	white wine vinegar	2 tbsp
2 tbsp	white wine	2 tbsp
¼ tsp	salt	¼ tsp
250 g	cherry tomatoes, skinned	8 oz

Heat the oil in a fireproof casserole that just fits the pork loin then, over medium heat, lightly brown the meat all over — about 6 minutes. Pour away the oil and add the fennel seeds, peppercorns, vinegar, wine and salt to the casserole. Cover and cook gently over low heat for 1 hour; check the level of the liquid occasionally, and add more vinegar and wine if necessary. About 10 minutes before the end of cooking, add the cherry tomatoes to the casserole.

Carefully remove the meat from the casserole and cut it into 5 mm (¼ inch) thick slices. Overlap the slices down the middle of a warmed serving dish and arrange the cherry tomatoes on either side. Skim off any fat from the juices in the casserole, then pour the juices over the meat together with the fennel seeds and green peppercorns.

Fillet Stuffed with Spinach, Ceps and Chestnuts

THIS DISH IS INTENDED TO BE SERVED COLD.

Serves 6
Working time: about 30 minutes
Total time: about 1 hour and 10 minutes·

Calories **190**
Protein **24g**
Cholesterol **70mg**
Total fat **8g**
Saturated fat **3g**
Sodium **270mg**

375 g	pork fillet in one piece	13 oz
500 g	fresh spinach, washed and stemmed	1 lb
½ tsp	coriander seeds	½ tsp
1 tsp	yellow mustard seeds	1 tsp
¼ tsp	ground mace	¼ tsp
½ tsp	salt	½ tsp
	freshly ground black pepper	
250 g	pork fillet or other lean pork, minced (page 11)	8 oz
60 g	fresh ceps, or 10 g (⅓ oz) dried ceps soaked for 20 minutes in warm water	2 oz
60 g	fresh chestnuts, or 15 g (½ oz) dried chestnuts soaked overnight	2 oz
1 tsp	safflower oil	1 tsp

Trim the fillet of all visible fat, sinew and transparent skin, and wipe it clean. Slit the fillet lengthwise with a sharp knife to a depth of half its thickness and flatten it out by beating it firmly (page 11, below).

Cook the spinach briefly in the water clinging to the leaves after washing; refresh under cold running water, squeeze hard to extract all possible moisture and chop finely.

Lightly toast the coriander and mustard seeds. Crush the coriander seeds in a mortar and combine with the mustard seeds, mace, salt and some pepper. If using dried mushrooms and chestnuts, strain and pat them dry.

Mix the minced pork with the spinach, coriander, mustard seeds and mace. Spread over the flattened-out fillet, and arrange the mushrooms and chestnuts along its length. Close up the fillet and tie round the circumference with string in six or eight places.

Preheat the oven to 190°C (375°F or Mark 5). Heat the oil in a wide, heavy or non-stick frying pan until hot, and brown the fillet all over, starting seam side down to seal the opening. Once the fillet is brown — 5 to 10 minutes — wrap it fairly tightly in baking foil and roast in the oven for 40 minutes.

Cool the fillet in the foil, then chill it in the refrigerator. To serve, cut two or three slices for each person.

SUGGESTED ACCOMPANIMENT: *red-leaved salad (such as oak-leaf lettuce or raddichio) or spinach.*

Roast Fillet with Pineapple Coulis

Serves 6
Working time: about 30 minutes
Total time: about 50 minutes

Calories **165**
Protein **20g**
Cholesterol **70mg**
Total fat **7g**
Saturated fat **3g**
Sodium **140mg**

750 g	pork fillet, trimmed of fat	1½ lb
¼ tsp	salt	¼ tsp
	freshly ground black pepper	
1	pineapple	1
	coriander leaves, finely chopped	

Preheat the oven to 180°C (350°F or Mark 4).

Season the fillet with the salt and a little freshly ground pepper, then wrap it in lightly greased aluminium foil. Place the fillet in an ovenproof casserole or roasting tin and cook it in the oven for 35 to 45 minutes, or until the juices run clear.

While the meat cooks, peel and core the pineapple. Liquidize the pulp in a food processor or blender, then pass it through a sieve. Refrigerate the pineapple coulis until you are ready to use it.

When the meat is cooked, unwrap it and add about a tablespoon of the juices collected in the foil to the pineapple coulis. Carve the meat into slices. Spread one or two spoonfuls of coulis on each serving plate and arrange the slices of meat round it. Sprinkle with the chopped coriander.

Grape Pork

Serves 8
Working time: about 45 minutes
Total time: about 2 hours and 15 minutes

Calories **245**
Protein **22g**
Cholesterol **80mg**
Total fat **8g**
Saturated fat **2g**
Sodium **315mg**

1 kg	boned leg of pork, fillet end, trimmed of fat	2 lb
750 g	green grapes, halved and seeded, or small seedless green grapes	1½ lb
1 tsp	virgin olive oil	1 tsp
½	onion, finely chopped	½
1	small garlic clove, crushed	1
125 g	fine fresh breadcrumbs	4 oz
¼ tsp	ground allspice	¼ tsp
2 tsp	Worcester sauce	2 tsp
½	beaten egg	½
1 tsp	salt	1 tsp
	freshly ground black pepper	
1 tbsp	arrowroot	1 tbsp
12.5 cl	dry Madeira	4 fl oz

Preheat the oven to 180°C (350°F or Mark 4). Lay out the pork on a work surface with its inner side facing up and cut in it five or six slits about 4 cm (1½ inches) deep, at equal intervals. Put 500 g (1 lb) of the grapes in a food processor and blend to a smooth purée; sieve the purée to strain the juice.

Heat the oil in a small non-stick frying pan and add the onion, garlic and 2 tablespoons of the grape juice. Cook over medium-low heat for 5 to 7 minutes or until the onion is softened, stirring occasionally. Tip the onion into a bowl and add the breadcrumbs, allspice, Worcester sauce, egg, ½ teaspoon of the salt and some pepper. Add another 2 tablespoons of the grape juice and mix to a soft, paste-like mixture.

Spread the paste over the pork, pushing some into the slits. Quarter about eight of the remaining grapes and press them into the stuffing. Reshape the joint and tie it securely into a rolled shape. Put the joint into a roasting bag and place in a roasting tin. Pour the remaining grape juice round the joint and tie the bag so that it is loosely closed. Make six 1 cm (½ inch) slits in the top of the bag, then roast for 1½ hours.

Cut open the top of the bag and lift out the pork on to a carving board. Cover the meat with foil and keep it warm while you finish the sauce.

Strain the cooking juices from the roasting bag into a saucepan. Dissolve the arrowroot in the Madeira and add to the pan. Bring the liquid to the boil, stirring constantly, and simmer until the sauce has thickened. Add the remaining grapes and salt, and some pepper, and heat through for 2 to 3 minutes. Carve the pork into thin slices and serve with the sauce.

SUGGESTED ACCOMPANIMENT: *salad of mixed lettuce.*

Eastern Scented Fillet

Serves 4
Working time: about 30 minutes
Total time: about 1 hour and 20 minutes

Calories **260**		
Protein **23g**		
Cholesterol **60mg**		
Total fat **9g**		
Saturated fat **3g**		
Sodium **185mg**		

400 g	pork fillet, trimmed of fat	14 oz
¼ tsp	salt	¼ tsp
½	cinnamon stick	½
2 tbsp	orange-flower water	2 tbsp
90 g	couscous	3 oz
60 g	dried apricots, soaked in hot water for 20 minutes	2 oz
30 g	raisins	1 oz
15 g	pine-nuts, lightly toasted	½ oz
½ tsp	ground coriander	½ tsp
¼ tsp	ground cumin	¼ tsp
1 tbsp	chopped fresh mint	1 tbsp
2 tbsp	chopped fresh tarragon	2 tbsp
	white pepper (optional)	
1 tsp	safflower oil	1 tsp
2 tsp	honey (preferably flower-scented)	2 tsp

Slit the fillet lengthwise with a sharp knife to a depth of half its thickness, and flatten it out as far as possible by beating with a mallet *(page 11, below)*. Season the cut surface with half of the salt.

Bring ¼ litre (8 fl oz) of water to the boil with the cin-namon and orange-flower water. Add the couscous to the liquid; stir for half a minute, cover tightly and remove from the heat. After 10 minutes the couscous will have absorbed all the liquid.

Drain the apricots and chop them roughly, then combine them in a mixing bowl with the raisins and pine-nuts. Remove the cinnamon and mix the cous-cous with the apricot mixture. Add the coriander, cumin, mint and tarragon; season with the remaining salt and some white pepper, if you are using it. Care-fully stuff the fillet with this mixture, reserving any excess filling for serving separately with the cooked meat. Close up the fillet and tie round its circum-ference in six to eight places with string.

Preheat the oven to 190°C (375°F or Mark 5). Heat the oil in a wide, heavy or preferably non-stick frying pan over medium heat, and brown the fillet all over, starting seam side down to seal the opening. Once the fillet is brown — 5 to 10 minutes — brush it all over with the honey and wrap it fairly tightly in foil. Roast the wrapped fillet for 20 minutes, then remove it from the oven and allow to rest for 5 minutes.

Open the foil packet and drain off the cooking juices into a small saucepan. Reduce the juices to a glaze and coat the fillet with the glaze. Remove the glazed fillet to a hot platter, slice and serve.

SUGGESTED ACCOMPANIMENTS: *couscous; tomato salad.*

Crépinettes in Mushroom Sauce

THE NAME CRÉPINETTE DERIVES FROM THE FRENCH WORD FOR CAUL, THE STOMACH MEMBRANE USED TO WRAP MEAT. DURING COOKING, THE CAUL MELTS AND KEEPS THE MEAT MOIST.

Serves 4
Working time: about 40 minutes
Total time: about 1 hour

Calories **280**
Protein **36g**
Cholesterol **75mg**
Total fat **13g**
Saturated fat **4g**
Sodium **415mg**

500 g	pork loin or fillet, trimmed of fat	1 lb
60 g	fresh chestnuts, or 30 g (1 oz) dried chestnuts soaked overnight	2 oz
2	pieces caul (about 20 g/⅔ oz)	2
100 g	brown cap mushrooms, or 15 g (½ oz) dried ceps soaked for 20 minutes in warm water	3½ oz
1 tbsp	cognac (optional)	1 tbsp
4	juniper berries, toasted and crushed	4
1 tsp	coriander seeds, toasted and crushed	1 tsp
½ tsp	yellow mustard seeds, toasted and crushed	½ tsp
1 tsp	salt	1 tsp
	freshly ground black pepper	
Mushroom sauce		
30 cl	unsalted veal stock (recipe, page 139)	½ pint
2 tbsp	red wine	2 tbsp
2	juniper berries, toasted and crushed	2
100 g	brown cap mushrooms, roughly sliced	3½ oz
2 tbsp	crème fraîche	2 tbsp
2 tbsp	fromage frais	2 tbsp

If you are using fresh chestnuts, score the tops and cook them in boiling water for 20 to 25 minutes, then drain them and peel off the skins. Soak the caul in lightly vinegared water for a few minutes to soften it (if the caul has been salted, soak in two or three changes of vinegared water). Spread the caul out flat and cut it into 12.5 cm (5 inch) squares — exact shaping is unimportant, as are occasional holes.

Preheat the oven to 200°C (400°F or Mark 6). Finely chop or mince the pork with the mushrooms. Cut each chestnut into three or four pieces, and mix these into the meat together with the cognac, if you are using it, the juniper, coriander, mustard seeds, salt and a little pepper. Mix well to distribute the spices evenly.

Divide the meat mixture into eight egg-shaped pieces of equal size and weight. Wrap each patty in a square of caul, overlapping the edges to ensure that the crépinette is completely enclosed.

Place the crépinettes in a shallow ovenproof dish and add the stock, wine and juniper berries that will be used for the sauce. Cook in the oven for about 25 minutes. Five minutes before the end of the cooking time, drain off the cooking juices into a saucepan and reduce to half the quantity over high heat. Add the mushrooms and the *crème fraîche* and cook for 2 to 3 minutes more. Stir in the *fromage frais*, pour the sauce round the crépinettes, and serve at once.

SUGGESTED ACCOMPANIMENT: *boiled asparagus.*

EDITOR'S NOTE: *For a more simple dish, the mushroom sauce may be omitted and the crépinettes can be grilled under low to medium heat for about 10 minutes per side.*

Sesame Schnitzels

TRADITIONAL WIENER SCHNITZELS ARE COATED IN BEATEN EGG AND WHITE BREADCRUMBS, THEN FRIED. THESE LOW-FAT SCHNITZELS HAVE A CRISP, NUTRITIOUS COATING MADE FROM EGG WHITE, GRANARY BREADCRUMBS AND SESAME SEEDS, AND ARE BAKED IN THE OVEN RATHER THAN FRIED.

Serves 4
Working time: about 20 minutes
Total time: about 30 minutes

Calories **420**
Protein **31g**
Cholesterol **60mg**
Total fat **21g**
Saturated fat **3g**
Sodium **470mg**

2	pork fillets (175 to 200 g/6 to 7 oz each)	2
⅛ tsp	salt	⅛ tsp
	freshly ground black pepper	
2	egg whites	2
150 g	dry granary breadcrumbs	5 oz
90 g	sesame seeds	3 oz
½ tsp	virgin olive oil	½ tsp
8	lemon slices, for garnish	8
12	fresh cranberries, cooked for 3 to 4 minutes in 1 tbsp water with 1 tbsp sugar, for garnish (optional)	12

Place a baking sheet in the oven and preheat the oven to 220°C (425°F or Mark 7). Trim off the tapered end of each piece of fillet and remove all visible fat and membrane. Cut each cylinder of meat into four rounds, then beat out the rounds to make eight escalopes (*page 12, above*). Sprinkle the meat on both sides with the salt and some pepper.

Put the egg whites in a shallow dish and whisk with a fork until they are lightly frothy. Mix the breadcrumbs and sesame seeds together and spread them out on a flat plate. Dip the pork escalopes one piece at a time in the egg whites, then coat them in the breadcrumb and sesame seed mixture, pressing it firmly on to the meat with your hands.

Brush the heated baking sheet with the olive oil and place the meat on it. Cook the schnitzels in the oven for 10 minutes until the surfaces are golden and crisp, turning once and pressing them hard with a fish slice to keep them flat.

Arrange the schnitzels on a warmed serving platter and garnish with the lemon slices and cranberries, if you are using them.

SUGGESTED ACCOMPANIMENT: *colourful mixed salad with a lemon-flavoured dressing.*

Cretan Roast Pork

Serves 6
Working time: about 15 minutes
Total time: about 1 hour and 15 minutes

Calories **190**			

Calories **190**
Protein **21g**
Cholesterol **70mg**
Total fat **9g**
Saturated fat **3g**
Sodium **335mg**

750 g	boned pork loin, trimmed of fat, rolled and tied	1½ lb
1 tbsp	finely chopped fresh oregano, or ½ tsp dried oregano	1 tbsp
1 tsp	salt	1 tsp
	freshly ground black pepper	
1 tbsp	virgin olive oil	1 tbsp
2	garlic cloves, finely chopped	2
250 g	plum or other ripe tomatoes, skinned, seeded and coarsely chopped	8 oz
12.5 cl	red wine	4 fl oz
2 tbsp	fresh lemon juice	2 tbsp

Preheat the oven to 200°C (400°F or Mark 6). Rub the surface of the joint with the oregano, salt and some pepper. Heat the oil in a wide, shallow fireproof dish over high heat and sear the joint briefly on all sides. Cook the garlic in the oil round the joint for a few seconds, then add the tomatoes, wine and lemon juice.

Bake, uncovered, for 1 hour, turning and basting the meat from time to time with the juices. Also check occasionally to make sure the tomato mixture does not burn, adding water if necessary.

Remove the joint to a large serving dish and coat it with the thick tomato paste before carving into slices. If any paste remains, serve it as an accompaniment.

SUGGESTED ACCOMPANIMENT: *steamed French beans.*

Lemon Pork

Serves 4
Working time: about 30 minutes
Total time: about 5 hours and 30 minutes
(includes marinating)

Calories **250**
Protein **33g**
Cholesterol **70mg**
Total fat **11g**
Saturated fat **4g**
Sodium **85mg**

500 g	boned pork loin, trimmed of fat	1 lb
1	lemon	1
	white pepper	
30 g	basil leaves	1 oz
1	garlic clove, crushed	1
3 tbsp	dry white wine	3 tbsp

Using a potato peeler, remove the rind from the lemon in long strips, working from top to bottom. Put the lemon strips into a pan of cold water, bring it to the boil, then drain and refresh the rind under cold running water. Drain well.

Cut the strips into threads that can be inserted into a larding needle. Weave some of the threads into the outer surface of the pork, then press the remainder of the threads on to the inner surface. Season the pork inside and out with a little white pepper. Roll up the pork and secure with string.

Squeeze the juice from the lemon. Tear the basil leaves into small pieces and place in a non-reactive dish with the garlic. Place the pork on top, pour the lemon juice over, cover and leave in a cool place, turning the pork occasionally, for 4 hours.

Heat the oven to 180°C (350°F or Mark 4). Lift the pork from the marinade and place on a large piece of aluminium foil. Fold the sides of the foil up, then pour in the marinade and the wine. Fold the foil loosely over the pork and seal the edges together firmly. Place the parcel on a baking sheet and cook in the oven until the pork is tender — about 40 minutes.

Transfer the pork to a warmed plate, cover and leave to rest. In a saucepan, boil the cooking juices until slightly thickened.

Carve the pork into slices, divide them among four warmed plates and spoon the juices round the meat.

SUGGESTED ACCOMPANIMENT: *steamed sliced courgettes.*

Oriental Pot Roast

Serves 12
Working time: about 30 minutes
Total time: about 2 hours and 45 minutes

Calories **220**
Protein **32g**
Cholesterol **70mg**
Total fat **8g**
Saturated fat **3g**
Sodium **310mg**

1.5 kg	prime leg, boned loin, or other lean roasting joint, trimmed of fat and tied into shape	3 lb
1 tbsp	safflower oil	1 tbsp
2 tbsp	very finely chopped fresh ginger root	2 tbsp
2 tbsp	very finely chopped garlic	2 tbsp
1 tbsp	very finely chopped fresh green chili pepper (caution, page 36)	1 tbsp
4 tbsp	rice wine or dry sherry	4 tbsp
2 tsp	brown sugar	2 tsp
4 tbsp	low-sodium soy sauce or shoyu	4 tbsp
2	sweet red peppers, each cut into 12 strips	2
24	baby sweetcorn	24
24	small spring onions	24

Brown the neatly tied joint well on all sides in a very hot, dry wok or heavy frying pan. It may seem to stick at first, but if you leave the "stuck" surface for a few seconds and the heat is high enough, the meat will soon loosen. Keep the wok unwashed for use later.

Heat the oil in a heavy-bottomed saucepan or fire-proof casserole, then add the ginger, garlic and chili pepper. Stir until the paste begins to brown, then add the rice wine or sherry and bring to the boil. Reduce the heat. Stir in the sugar and soy sauce, then place the browned joint in the casserole and turn it in the mixture so that all sides are coated. Ensure the heat is very low, cover the pot and simmer for 2¼ hours.

About 15 minutes before serving, stir-fry first the red pepper strips, then the baby sweetcorn and finally the spring onions in the wok or frying pan over fierce heat. Remove each batch to a bowl after stir-frying. All the

vegetables should have softened slightly and be flecked with black, but still crisp.

When the meat is ready, remove the string and slice into 12 portions. Lay the slices on a serving platter. If the liquid in the casserole has not reduced to a dark, glossy syrup, skim off any surface fat and reduce the liquid over high heat. Toss the vegetables in this syrup and make sure they are thoroughly heated through, then spoon them over the pork and serve immediately.

SUGGESTED ACCOMPANIMENTS: *steamed rice; steamed slices of Chinese cabbage in oyster sauce.*

Green Peppercorn Fillet

Serves 4
Working time: about 35 minutes
Total time: about 1 hour and 20 minutes

Calories **180**
Protein **19g**
Cholesterol **60mg**
Total fat **9g**
Saturated fat **3g**
Sodium **240mg**

350 g	pork fillet, trimmed of fat	12 oz
125 g	button mushrooms	4 oz
15 g	shallots	½ oz
1 tsp	virgin olive oil	1 tsp
3 tbsp	fresh lemon juice	3 tbsp
½ tsp	salt	½ tsp
60 g	fine French beans, trimmed	2 oz
1 tsp	dried green peppercorns, coarsely crushed	1 tsp
1 tbsp	chopped fresh marjoram, or 1 tsp dried marjoram	1 tbsp
20 cl	unsalted chicken stock (recipe, page 139)	7 fl oz
20 cl	dry white wine	7 fl oz

Preheat the oven to 190°C (375°F or Mark 5).

Cut a lengthwise slit about half way into the pork fillet, then open the pork like a book and place it, cut side down, on a board. Cover with a piece of plastic film and pound with a wooden mallet until the pork has a rectangular shape and is about 1 cm (½ inch) thick (*page 11, below*).

Chop the mushrooms and shallots in a food processor. Heat the oil in a small non-stick frying pan and add the mushrooms and shallots and 1 tablespoon of the lemon juice. Cook over moderate heat for about 5 minutes, stirring frequently, until quite dry. Remove from the heat and stir in the salt. Set aside.

Blanch the beans in boiling water for 3 minutes. Drain the beans and refresh them under cold running water, then drain them well again and dry them on paper towels.

Spread the mushroom mixture over the pork, leaving about 5 mm (¼ inch) clear on all sides. Sprinkle the peppercorns evenly over the mushroom mixture, then arrange the beans neatly on top, parallel to the long edges of the meat. Press the beans gently into the mushroom mixture, and sprinkle over the marjoram.

Roll up the pork from a long side and tie into shape in several places with string. Place the stuffed pork roll in a small roasting tin and pour over the chicken stock, half of the white wine and the remaining lemon juice. Roast the meat for about 45 minutes in the oven,

basting two or three times with the cooking juices.

Remove the pork roll from the oven and keep it warm while you make the gravy. On top of the stove, deglaze the roasting tin with the remaining wine, stirring to mix in the sediment from the bottom of the tin. Strain into a gravy boat. Put the pork on a carving board, cut away the string and slice the meat thinly. Arrange the slices on a heated serving plate, and serve accompanied by the gravy.

Fillet Persillé with Carrot Purée

Serves 4
Working time: about 40 minutes
Total time: about 50 minutes

Calories **230**
Protein **22g**
Cholesterol **75mg**
Total fat **9g**
Saturated fat **4g**
Sodium **380mg**

500 g	pork fillet, trimmed of fat	1 lb
½ tsp	salt	½ tsp
	freshly ground black pepper	
2 tbsp	Dijon mustard	2 tbsp
4 tbsp	finely chopped parsley	4 tbsp
30 g	fine dry white breadcrumbs	1 oz
	Carrot purée	
350 g	carrots	12 oz
4 tbsp	fresh orange juice	4 tbsp
7 g	unsalted butter, chilled and cut into tiny cubes	¼ oz

Preheat the oven to 200°C (400°F or Mark 6). Wipe the fillet dry and season it with the salt and some pepper. Sear it in a hot, dry non-stick frying pan until it is brown all over. Brush the fillet with the mustard and sprinkle with the parsley on all sides, then carefully roll it in the breadcrumbs so it is evenly coated. Place on a wire rack over a baking tin and roast for 30 to 40 minutes, until the meat is cooked and the crumbs are brown.

Steam the carrots until tender, then purée them with the orange juice, either in a food processor or by passing them through a sieve. Heat the purée through slowly in a small pan, gradually beating in the butter.

Let the cooked fillet rest for 10 minutes, then carve it into thick slices and serve with the carrot purée.

SUGGESTED ACCOMPANIMENTS: *new potatoes; French beans.*

EDITOR'S NOTE: *The fillet may also be eaten cold, cut into thin slices and served with a vinaigrette made with 2 tablespoons finely chopped carrot, 3 tablespoons each white wine vinegar and fresh orange juice, and 4 tablespoons safflower oil.*

Herbed Roast Fillet of Pork with Three Purées

Serves 4
Working (and total) time: about 40 minutes

Calories **285**
Protein **25g**
Cholesterol **80mg**
Total fat **12g**
Saturated fat **5g**
Sodium **420mg**

500 g	pork fillet, trimmed of fat	1 lb
15 g	unsalted butter	½ oz
½ tsp	salt	½ tsp
	freshly ground black pepper	
1 tsp	chopped tarragon	1 tsp
1½ tsp	chopped flat-leaf parsley	1½ tsp
1 tbsp	safflower oil	1 tbsp
½	lemon, juice only	½
¾ litre	unsalted chicken stock (recipe, page 139) or water	1¼ pints
350 g	carrots, peeled and roughly chopped	12 oz
175 g	potatoes, peeled and roughly chopped	6 oz
175 g	celeriac, peeled and roughly chopped	6 oz
175 g	beetroot, peeled and roughly chopped	6 oz
175 g	new white turnips, peeled and roughly chopped	6 oz
12.5 cl	milk	4 fl oz
2	chervil sprigs, torn into pieces	2

Preheat the oven to 230°C (450°F or Mark 8).
With a sharp knife, cut a deep lengthwise slit in the fillet to within about 1 cm (½ inch) of the opposite side.

Spread the butter inside the pocket, season with the salt and some pepper, and stuff the pocket with the tarragon and parsley. Secure the pocket by tying string round the fillet at intervals of about 4 cm (1½ inches). Heat the oil in a heavy frying pan over medium heat and brown the fillet all over. Remove the fillet from the pan, put it on a large piece of foil, pour the lemon juice over the meat, then wrap loosely.

Put the fillet in the oven to cook for about 25 minutes. Divide the stock or water among three pans and bring to the boil; cook the carrots in the first pan, the potato and celeriac in the second and the beetroot and turnip in the third, until soft.

When the vegetables are soft, drain them, reserving the cooking liquid. In a food processor, purée the carrots with a little of their reserved cooking liquid, the beetroot and turnip also with a little reserved liquid, and the potato and celeriac with the milk. Return each purée to its cooking pan.

When the fillet is cooked, warm the purées gently over low heat. Cut the fillet into thin slices, and either arrange these on a large serving plate and hand the purées separately, or divide them among individual dining plates with the three purées spooned round them. Garnish with the pieces of chervil.

EDITOR'S NOTE: *The purées can be prepared in advance and refrigerated until required.*

2 *Under the lid of an Oriental steaming basket, meatballs of pork and burghul (recipe, page 97) are evenly arranged on the bamboo latticework.*

Balancing the Flavours

Cooking meat in a liquid precipitates a gradual exchange of benefits — as the meat's juices are released, the meat in turn absorbs the flavours in the liquid around it. In the recipes in this chapter, the disparate ingredients — meat, vegetables, fruits, herbs, spices, liquids — all contribute to this transaction, challenging the cook to create from their unique characteristics a harmonious whole. The method may be as simple as cooking all the ingredients together for a specified time, as is the case with the Indian stew on page 80. More often, the process involves several stages to allow for the different cooking times of the various constituents, but the aim is always the same: a balanced interplay of flavours and textures in which no one element overwhelms or detracts from another.

Poaching and braising are both methods customarily employed to cook tougher cuts of meat that require lengthy cooking to break down their connective tissue, but they are equally appropriate to the fillets and loin cuts that feature in many of the recipes that follow. In poaching, the meat is completely immersed in a liquid and cooked over low heat on top of the stove. Because boiling causes meat to become tough and stringy, it is important to maintain the liquid at a constant simmer — the surface should be just trembling, with bubbles drifting slowly up. And any fat that melts out of the meat during cooking should be carefully skimmed off.

Braises require less liquid, and may be cooked either on the stove or in the oven. When the meat is cut into pieces, it is usually described as a stew. Before the liquid is added, the meat is often seared at a high temperature — large cuts in the oven, small cuts and pieces on the stove — to give its surface an appetizing brown crust. It may also be tenderized in a marinade which is later added to the cooking liquid, and larger cuts may be stuffed. The cooking liquid itself is often stock, wine or water, but beer *(page 75)*, cider *(page 78)* and even milk *(page 67)* are all appropriate liquids for pork.

A number of recipes in this chapter call for a steamer, a pan with one or two perforated containers in which the food is cooked by steam rising from the boiling liquid beneath it. Steaming is particularly suitable for delicate foods such as the minced pork balls with onion and burghul opposite. In another recipe, stuffed pork steaks are steamed over boiling stock and fennel *(page 95)*; and in the couscous dish on page 96, the pork is cooked with vegetables over boiling water and ginger while the couscous steams in the second container above them — a progressive transfusion of flavours that elevates the final assembly into far more than the sum of its parts.

White Cabbage Pork

Serves 4
Working time: about 30 minutes
Total time: about 7 hours and 30 minutes (includes marinating)

Calories **250**
Protein **23g**
Cholesterol **70mg**
Total fat **11g**
Saturated fat **3g**
Sodium **185mg**

500 g	boned pork loin, trimmed of fat	1 lb
1½ tsp	caraway seeds	1½ tsp
30 cl	apple juice	½ pint
1 tbsp	safflower oil	1 tbsp
1	small onion, finely chopped	1
400 g	white cabbage, shredded	14 oz
¼ tsp	salt	¼ tsp
	white pepper	
1	small red-skinned apple, for garnish	1
	dill sprigs, for garnish	

Sprinkle half the caraway seeds over the inside of the pork, roll it up and tie it with string. Place the pork in a non-reactive bowl, sprinkle the remaining caraway seeds over, then pour in the apple juice. Cover and leave in a cool place for 6 hours, turning occasionally.

Preheat the oven to 170°C (325°F or Mark 3).

Remove the pork from the bowl and pat it dry; reserve the apple juice. Heat a heavy fireproof casserole, add the oil and brown the pork evenly over high heat. Transfer the meat to a plate. Add the onion to the casserole and cook, stirring frequently, over low heat for 3 to 4 minutes. Add the cabbage in batches and cook each batch, stirring frequently, for 2 to 3 minutes; remove each batch to a large bowl before sautéing the next one. When all the cabbage is cooked, stir the contents of the bowl to distribute the onion evenly. Set the pork on a layer of cabbage and onion in the casserole and surround it with the remaining cabbage and onion. Bring the reserved apple juice to the boil, add the salt and some pepper, then pour it over the pork.

Cover the casserole tightly and cook in the oven until the pork is tender — about 45 minutes. Transfer the pork to a warmed plate, cover and leave to rest for about 10 minutes. Meanwhile, core and slice the apple.

Carve the pork into slices. Arrange the cabbage on a warm dish, place the pork on top and spoon the cooking juices over. Garnish with the dill and apple.

Loin Cooked in Milk

Serves 4
Working time: about 20 minutes
Total time: about 1 hour and 10 minutes

Calories **265**
Protein **35g**
Cholesterol **70mg**
Total fat **11g**
Saturated fat **5g**
Sodium **135mg**

500 g	boned pork loin, trimmed of fat, rolled and tied	1 lb
1	onion, finely chopped	1
3 tbsp	unsalted veal stock (recipe, page 139) or water	3 tbsp
2	fresh bay leaves, broken	2
1	small thyme sprig, or ¼ tsp dried thyme	1
1	parsley sprig	1
¼ tsp	salt	¼ tsp
	freshly ground black pepper	
35 cl	skimmed milk	12 fl oz

In a heavy-bottomed saucepan or fireproof casserole, gently simmer the onion in the stock or water until it is soft and the liquid evaporated — 3 to 4 minutes. Add the bay leaves, thyme and parsley. Place the pork on top, season with the salt and some pepper, then gradually pour in the milk. Increase the heat and bring the liquid to the boil, then simmer, covered, for 45 minutes to 1 hour, until the pork is just tender and the milk well reduced — a skin should form on the surface.

Lift the pork out carefully with a slotted spoon and keep it warm. Continue to simmer the sauce, if necessary, until only about 6 tablespoons remain.

Carve the pork into slices and divide it among four warmed plates. Remove the herbs from the sauce and spoon a quarter of the sauce on to each plate.

SUGGESTED ACCOMPANIMENT: *new potatoes with parsley.*

Rolled Escalopes with Aubergines

Serves 4
Working time: about 1 hour
Total time: about 3 hours (includes marinating)

Calories **168**
Protein **20g**
Cholesterol **65mg**
Total fat **20g**
Saturated fat **3g**
Sodium **205mg**

4	pork escalopes (about 90 g / 3 oz each), very thinly sliced	4
½ tsp	finely chopped fresh sage	½ tsp
1 tsp	finely chopped fresh thyme	1 tsp
	freshly ground black pepper	
2	large aubergines (about 250 g / 8 oz each)	2
1 tsp	salt	1 tsp
1½ tbsp	virgin olive oil	1½ tbsp
2	garlic cloves, finely chopped	2
500 g	ripe plum tomatoes, skinned, seeded and chopped, or 300 g (10 oz) canned plum tomatoes, drained and chopped	1 lb

Beat out the escalopes to tenderize them *(page 12, above, Step 2)*. Sprinkle the meat evenly on both sides with the sage, thyme and a little pepper, and leave it to absorb the flavours for 30 minutes to 1 hour.

Meanwhile, cut the stems off the aubergines and peel off half the skin in alternate lengthwise strips. Cut the aubergines diagonally into 5 mm (¼ inch) thick slices; sprinkle the slices evenly with ½ teaspoon of the salt and leave them to drain in a colander for at least 30 minutes.

Preheat the oven to 220°C (425°F or Mark 7). Rinse the aubergines well under cold running water, then press each slice firmly between your hands so that the spongy texture is broken down and the appearance becomes waxy. Dry the slices on paper towels.

Cover each escalope with a single layer of aubergine slices, then roll each escalope up tightly, beginning at one of its shorter edges, into a neat, chubby sausage and secure with wooden toothpicks.

Arrange the rolled escalopes in a single layer in an ovenproof gratin dish, brush them with half of the oil and bake, uncovered, for 30 minutes, turning once so that all sides are evenly coloured.

Meanwhile, heat the remaining oil in a heavy frying pan. Cut any remaining aubergine slices into small dice and fry these with the garlic until the aubergine is well coloured. Add the tomatoes and about half the remaining salt, and continue cooking until the mixture is well reduced and thick — about 10 minutes.

When the rolled escalopes are golden, reduce the oven temperature to 190°C (375°F or Mark 5). Pour the tomato mixture over the meat, cover the dish with foil and braise for 1 hour.

Remove the meat rolls to a warm serving plate, take out the toothpicks and trim the ends of the rolls to expose the spirals of aubergine. Sprinkle the rolls with the remaining salt. Transfer the contents of the gratin dish to a saucepan, and reduce over medium heat until thick and well mixed. Spoon the sauce over the meat before serving.

SUGGESTED ACCOMPANIMENTS: *steamed saffron rice; salad of crisp leaves.*

Red Cabbage Pork

Serves 4
Working time: about 30 minutes
Total time: about 2 hours

Calories **310**	750 g	boned pork loin	1 ½ lb
Protein **37g**	1 tbsp	safflower oil	1 tbsp
Cholesterol **110mg**	1	onion, finely chopped	1
Total fat **13g**	500 g	red cabbage, shredded	1 lb
Saturated fat **4g**	350 g	firm pears, peeled and thickly sliced	12 oz
Sodium **170mg**	3	cloves	3
	1 tsp	sugar	1 tsp
	3 tbsp	fresh lemon juice	3 tbsp
	2	strips lemon rind, each about 5 cm (2 inches) long	2

Preheat the oven to 170°C (325°F or Mark 3). Trim the loin of all visible fat and roll it, tying it with string in several places. Heat the oil in a heavy fireproof casserole over high heat, add the pork and cook for about 3 minutes, turning the pork so that it browns evenly.

Transfer the meat to a plate and set it aside.

Reduce the heat, add the onion to the casserole and cook, stirring frequently and scraping up the caramelized juices from the base of the casserole, until softened — 3 to 4 minutes. Add the cabbage in batches and cook, stirring frequently, for about 2 minutes per batch. Remove each batch to a plate before frying the next one.

Mix the cabbage and onion, pears, cloves and sugar together in a bowl, then make a thick bed of about half of the cabbage mixture in the bottom of the casserole. Add the lemon juice and strips of lemon rind. Place the pork on top and pack the remaining cabbage mixture round the meat and over the top. Cover the casserole and cook in the oven for about 1 hour and 20 minutes.

Transfer the pork to a warmed plate, cover and leave to rest. Spoon off the juices from the cabbage and boil until slightly reduced. Carve the pork into slices and divide among four warmed plates. Add the cabbage and pear mixture and spoon the juices over.

Mango Pork

Serves 8
Working time: about 35 minutes
Total time: about 2 hours and 15 minutes

Calories **270**
Protein **33g**
Cholesterol **70mg**
Total fat **13g**
Saturated fat **4g**
Sodium **115mg**

1 kg	boned pork loin, trimmed of fat, rolled and tied	2 lb
1 tbsp	virgin olive oil	1 tbsp
½	onion, finely chopped	½
1	carrot, chopped	1
1	stick celery, chopped	1
1	garlic clove, finely chopped	1
1 tbsp	chopped fresh ginger root	1 tbsp
1 tbsp	coriander seeds	1 tbsp
12	cardamom pods, lightly crushed to open	12
1 tsp	cumin seeds	1 tsp
½ tsp	black peppercorns	½ tsp
½	cinnamon stick	½
1	dried chili pepper, halved (caution, page 36)	1
30 cl	unsalted chicken stock (recipe, page 139)	½ pint
15 cl	dry sherry	¼ pint
1	ripe mango, peeled, stoned and chopped	1
½	lemon, juice only (optional)	½
½	cucumber, halved lengthwise and thinly sliced, for garnish	½
15 g	coriander sprigs, stalks removed, leaves torn into small pieces, for garnish	½ oz

Preheat the oven to 180°C (350°F or Mark 4). Heat the oil in a medium-sized deep fireproof casserole over medium-low heat. Add the chopped onion, carrot,

celery, garlic and ginger. Cover and cook gently until softened — 5 to 7 minutes — stirring occasionally.

Add the coriander, cardamom, cumin, peppercorns, cinnamon and chili pepper, and stir to mix with the vegetables. Place the pork on top. Pour in the stock and sherry and bring to the boil, then cover tightly and transfer to the oven. Braise for about 1½ hours.

Remove the pork from the casserole and scrape off any spices or vegetables that have stuck to it. Wrap it in foil and set aside while you make the sauce.

Strain the cooking liquid into a saucepan, pressing down on the vegetables and spices in the sieve to extract all their flavourings; discard the contents of the sieve. Put the mango in a food processor with about half of the strained cooking liquid and blend to a purée. Press the purée through the sieve into the saucepan containing the remaining cooking liquid and stir to mix. Add the lemon juice if you are using it, then gently reheat the sauce.

Slice the pork thinly and arrange on hot plates with the sauce poured round or spooned over. Garnish with the cucumber slices and the coriander leaves.

Sorrel Paupiettes

Serves 4
Working (and total) time: about 50 minutes

Calories **235**
Protein **35g**
Cholesterol **85mg**
Total fat **14g**
Saturated fat **4g**
Sodium **280mg**

300 g	pork escalopes (2 large or 4 small), trimmed of fat	10 oz
175 g	neck end or other lean pork for mincing	6 oz
30 g	fresh sorrel leaves, deveined	1 oz
1	small bunch each of fresh sage, thyme and marjoram	1
½ tsp	fresh green peppercorns, or bottled green peppercorns rinsed and drained	½ tsp
½ tsp	salt	½ tsp
	freshly ground black pepper	
15 g	fresh green shelled pistachio nuts	½ oz
1 tsp	safflower oil	1 tsp
7 g	unsalted butter	¼ oz
¼ litre	unsalted chicken stock (recipe, page 139)	8 fl oz
Mustard and sorrel sauce		
¼ tsp	arrowroot	¼ tsp
1 tbsp	unsalted chicken stock (recipe, page 139) or water	1 tbsp
75 g	fromage frais	2½ oz
2 tsp	grainy mustard	2 tsp
¼ tsp	salt	¼ tsp
15 g	fresh sorrel leaves, shredded	½ oz

Beat out the escalopes until double their original size (page 12, above, Step 2); if using large escalopes, cut them in half.

Plunge the sorrel leaves into boiling water, then refresh them immediately under cold running water. Dry them carefully on a tea towel or paper towels.

Cover one side of each escalope with sorrel leaves.

In a food processor, mince the lean pork with the sage, thyme, marjoram, peppercorns, salt and some pepper. Turn the mixture into a non-stick pan and cook for about 5 minutes, stirring continuously. Allow to cool slightly, then spread a quarter of the mixture on to the leaf-coated side of each escalope. Arrange a quarter of the pistachio nuts towards one end of each escalope and roll up the meat into paupiettes, starting at the pistachioed end. The bundles should hold together without tying, but if not, secure gently with string.

Heat the oil and butter together in a heavy frying pan with a lid. Place the paupiettes carefully in the pan, seam side down, and brown them gently over medium heat for about 6 minutes, covering if the meat is in danger of burning, and turning the paupiettes from time to time once the seam has sealed. Meanwhile, warm the stock over low heat.

Remove the paupiettes and wipe the pan surface with paper towels to remove residual fat. Replace the meat in the pan and add the stock. Simmer very gently (a fast bubble will toughen the meat) for a further 5 minutes, until the meat is tender.

Remove the paupiettes from the pan, discard any string used, and keep the paupiettes warm while you make the sauce. Dissolve the arrowroot in the stock or water, and stir the mixture into the cooking liquid in the pan. Cook gently for a minute or two until slightly thickened and clear. Off the heat, beat in the *fromage frais* and mustard. Season with the salt, then add the meat and warm through over very low heat. Immediately before serving, stir in the shredded sorrel. Serve hot, slicing each paupiette on presentation, if you wish.

SUGGESTED ACCOMPANIMENTS: *new or jacket-baked potatoes; lightly cooked leaf spinach.*

EDITOR'S NOTE: *If sorrel is not available, young spinach leaves may be used instead.*

Loin Chops with Mushrooms and Sherry

Serves 4
Working time: about 35 minutes
Total time: about 1 hour and 20 minutes

Calories **270**
Protein **36g**
Cholesterol **70mg**
Total fat **12g**
Saturated fat **5g**
Sodium **300mg**

4	loin chops (125 to 150 g/ 4½ to 5 oz each), trimmed of fat	4
½ tsp	salt	½ tsp
	freshly ground black pepper	
1	onion, finely chopped	1
1	garlic clove, very finely chopped	1
500 g	button mushrooms, finely chopped	1 lb
8 cl	dry sherry	3 fl oz
2	large sorrel leaves, deveined, cut into thin strips	2
75 g	fromage frais	2½ oz

Season the chops with the salt and a little pepper, then brown them well on both sides in a non-stick frying pan. Remove them to a heavy, fireproof casserole.

Sweat the onion and garlic, covered, in the frying pan until they are soft but not coloured. Add them to the chops in the casserole.

Put the mushrooms into the frying pan, turn up the heat and stir as they begin to cook. When they have given up their juice, add the sherry and boil vigorously for 2 minutes. Transfer them to the casserole.

Bring the contents of the casserole to the boil, then reduce the heat, cover, and leave to cook at a lively simmer for 45 minutes or until the chops are tender. Remove the chops, scraping off and returning any pieces of vegetable to the casserole, and keep warm.

Increase the heat under the mushroom mixture, and boil to reduce the liquid completely. Stir in the sorrel leaves, then remove the casserole from the heat and stir in the *fromage frais*. Serve the chops immediately on individual plates, with a large spoonful of the mushroom mixture on top of each chop.

SUGGESTED ACCOMPANIMENT: *steamed broccoli.*

EDITOR'S NOTE: *If sorrel is not available, substitute spinach and stir in 1 teaspoon of lemon juice with the fromage frais.*

Pork Cooked Like Game

Serves 4
Working time: about 30 minutes
Total time: about 1 day (includes marinating)

Calories **220**
Protein **22g**
Cholesterol **70mg**
Total fat **7g**
Saturated fat **3g**
Sodium **115mg**

500 g	boned pork loin, trimmed of fat and rolled	1 lb
30 g	dried ceps	1 oz
1	onion, sliced	1
	Juniper marinade	
1	small onion, finely chopped	1
1	small carrot, diced	1
10	juniper berries	10
4	black peppercorns, lightly crushed	4
1	fresh bay leaf, broken in half	1
1	small rosemary sprig	1
1	thyme sprig	1
1	parsley sprig	1
30 cl	red wine	½ pt

To prepare the marinade, scatter the onion and carrot in the bottom of a non-reactive dish. Lay the pork on top, add the juniper berries, peppercorns, bay leaf, rosemary, thyme and parsley, then pour the wine over. Cover the dish and leave it in a cool place for about 24 hours, turning the pork occasionally.

Pour 30 cl (½ pint) of boiling water over the mushrooms and leave them to soak for 20 minutes. Strain the mushrooms and reserve the liquid.

Preheat the oven to 170°C (325°F or Mark 3). Lift the pork from the marinade; reserve the marinade. On top of the stove, heat a heavy or non-stick fireproof casserole; add the pork and cook over high heat, turning the pork so that it browns evenly all over. Transfer the pork to a plate.

Add the sliced onion to the casserole and cook over low heat, stirring frequently and scraping the caramelized meat juices from the bottom of the casserole, until slightly softened — 2 to 3 minutes. Return the pork to the casserole, add the mushrooms, then pour over the mushroom-soaking liquid and the marinade so that the pork is almost covered. Increase the heat and bring the liquid to simmering point.

Cover the casserole tightly, transfer it to the oven, and cook for 40 to 45 minutes. When the meat is cooked, transfer it to a warmed plate, cover and leave to rest in a low oven.

Strain the cooking liquid; discard the bay leaf and herb sprigs but reserve the vegetables. Skim off any fat from the surface of the liquid, then reduce the liquid by about three quarters.

Carve the pork into slices. Accompany each serving with the reserved vegetables and the reduced sauce.

Chops with Spiced Orange Sauce

Serves 4
Working time: about 20 minutes
Total time: about 35 minutes

Calories **200**
Protein **21g**
Cholesterol **70mg**
Total fat **8g**
Saturated fat **3g**
Sodium **275mg**

4	boneless pork loin chops (about 125 g/ 4 oz each), trimmed of fat	4
2	shallots, finely chopped	2
1	small sweet green pepper, seeded, deribbed and cut into thin strips	1
¼ tsp	ground cinnamon	¼ tsp
⅛ tsp	ground cloves	⅛ tsp
3	large oranges, juice and grated rind of two, one peeled and thinly sliced	3
1 tbsp	soft brown sugar	1 tbsp
2 tsp	arrowroot	2 tsp
½ tsp	salt	½ tsp
	freshly ground black pepper	

In a large non-stick frying pan, brown the chops over high heat for 3 minutes, turning once. Add the shallots and green pepper and continue to cook, stirring, for 2 minutes. Stir in the cinnamon and cloves.

Put the orange juice into a measuring jug and make the liquid up to ¼ litre (8 fl oz) with water. Add the liquid to the pan together with the orange rind and sugar. Bring to the boil, then reduce the heat and simmer for about 10 minutes, until the chops are tender.

Using a slotted spoon, remove the pork chops to a serving plate and keep warm. Add the orange slices to the pan and heat through.

In a small bowl or cup, mix the arrowroot with 2 tablespoons of cold water, then add to the pan and stir well until the sauce thickens. Season with the salt and some freshly ground pepper. Spoon the orange sauce round the pork to serve.

Pork Carbonnade

Serves 8
Working time: about 40 minutes
Total time: about 2 hours and 20 minutes

Calories **480**
Protein **38g**
Cholesterol **70mg**
Total fat **25g**
Saturated fat **6g**
Sodium **550mg**

1 kg	lean pork shoulder, trimmed of fat and cut into bite-sized pieces	2 lb
4 tbsp	plain wholemeal flour	4 tbsp
60 g	polyunsaturated margarine	2 oz
3 tbsp	safflower oil	3 tbsp
3	large onions, halved and sliced	3
3	garlic cloves, crushed	3
45 cl	unsalted chicken stock (recipe, page 139)	¾ pint
45 cl	light ale	¾ pint
3 tsp	wine vinegar	3 tsp
1 tsp	salt	1 tsp
	freshly ground black pepper	
1	bouquet garni	1
8	slices French bread, 1 cm (½ inch) thick	8
1½ tbsp	grainy mustard	1½ tbsp
3 tbsp	chopped parsley	3 tbsp
90 g	reduced-fat Cheddar cheese, grated	3 oz
	fresh bay leaves, for garnish	

Preheat the oven to 180°C (350°F or Mark 4). Toss the pork in the flour until the pieces are thoroughly coated. Heat half of the margarine with the oil in a large saucepan, and gently cook the onions and two of the crushed garlic cloves for 3 minutes.

Using a slotted spoon, transfer the onions to a casserole. Add the pork to the pan, reserving any excess flour. Fry the pork over fairly high heat, turning until the cubes are sealed all over; stir in any remaining flour and cook for 1 minute. Gradually add the stock and light ale and bring almost to the boil, stirring all the time. Add the vinegar, salt and some pepper, pour the mixture over the onions in the casserole, then add the bouquet garni. Cover the casserole and cook in the oven for 1½ hours.

Meanwhile, prepare the bread topping. Toast the slices of French bread on one side only. Mix the remaining margarine with the mustard, 2 tablespoons of the chopped parsley and the remaining crushed garlic clove. Spread the mixture over the untoasted sides of the bread.

At the end of its cooking time, remove the casserole from the oven and discard the bouquet garni. Arrange the slices of bread, toasted sides down, on top of the casserole, pushing each slice into the pork mixture to moisten it. Sprinkle with the grated Cheddar cheese, then cook, uncovered, in the oven for a further 25 minutes, until the topping is golden. Sprinkle the top with the remaining chopped parsley, garnish with the fresh bay leaves and serve.

Light Gumbo

Serves 4
Working time: about 30 minutes
Total time: about 2 hours

Calories **290**			
Protein **40g**	350 g	lean pork, trimmed of fat and cut into 1 cm (½ inch) cubes	12 oz
Cholesterol **145mg**	250 g	cooked prawns, unpeeled	8 oz
Total fat **13g**	3	parsley sprigs	3
Saturated fat **5g**	½ tsp	black peppercorns	½ tsp
Sodium **370mg**	½ tsp	salt	½ tsp
	1	onion, finely chopped	1
	1	garlic clove, crushed	1
	250 g	okra, trimmed and cut into 2.5 cm (1 inch) slices	8 oz
	1	fresh green chili pepper, finely chopped (caution, page 36)	1
	250 g	tomatoes, skinned, seeded and cut into fine strips	8 oz
	3 tbsp	finely chopped fresh coriander, or 3 tbsp chopped parsley plus 2 tbsp fresh lime juice	3 tbsp

Remove the heads and shells from the prawns and set the flesh aside. Bring the heads and shells to the boil in 1 litre (1¾ pints) of water with the parsley sprigs and peppercorns, cover and simmer for 20 minutes. Strain the prawn stock through a sieve and set aside; discard the solids.

Brown the meat in a dry non-stick frying pan, stir in the salt, then add the onion and garlic and cook for about 5 minutes, until the onion has softened. Transfer the contents of the frying pan to a saucepan, add the stock and bring to the boil. Cover and leave to simmer until the meat is very tender — about 1½ hours.

Toss the okra in a wok or dry non-stick frying pan over high heat until it is charred in places but still green and crisp. Stir in the chili pepper and cook briefly, then tip the mixture into the stew. Add the tomatoes, coriander, or parsley and lime juice, and the prawns. Bring the stew quickly to the boil and serve.

SUGGESTED ACCOMPANIMENT: *crusty bread or boiled rice.*

EDITOR'S NOTE: Gumbo is usually served in bowls as a soup-stew and eaten with spoons.

Pork Stroganoff

NAMED AFTER A 19TH-CENTURY RUSSIAN DIPLOMAT, STROGANOFF
IS TRADITIONALLY A BEEF DISH WITH ONIONS AND MUSHROOMS IN
A THICK SOURED CREAM SAUCE. IN THIS LIGHT ADAPTATION FOR
PORK, YOGURT REPLACES THE SOURED CREAM.

Serves 4
Working (and total) time: about 25 minutes

Calories **250**
Protein **24g**
Cholesterol **70mg**
Total fat **14g**
Saturated fat **4g**
Sodium **190mg**

500 g	pork fillet, trimmed of fat and cut into thin strips	1 lb
1½ tbsp	safflower oil	1½ tbsp
1	large onion, quartered, thinly sliced	1
175 g	button mushrooms, sliced	6 oz
2 tbsp	plain wholemeal flour	2 tbsp
30 cl	unsalted chicken stock (recipe, page 139)	½ pint
1 tbsp	tomato paste	1 tbsp
1 tsp	fresh lemon juice	1 tsp
¼ tsp	salt	¼ tsp
	freshly ground black pepper	
60 g	thick Greek yogurt	2 oz

Heat the oil in a large frying pan until it is smoking, add the pork strips and onion and cook for 3 minutes, stirring frequently, until the pork is browned all over. Add the mushrooms and cook for a further minute, stirring.

Add the flour to the pan and mix well, then gradually stir in the stock and bring to the boil, stirring all the time. Reduce the heat and simmer for 2 minutes, then stir in the tomato paste, lemon juice, salt and some pepper. Heat the mixture through gently for 2 minutes.

Remove the pan from the heat, stir in the yogurt and serve immediately.

SUGGESTED ACCOMPANIMENT: *green or wholewheat tagliatelle.*

Pork Hotpot

Serves 8
Working time: about 40 minutes
Total time: about 4 hours and 30 minutes (includes soaking)

Calories **365**			
Protein **25g**	1 kg	pork fillet, trimmed of fat and cut into chunks	2 lb
Cholesterol **70mg**	¾ litre	dry cider	1¼ pints
Total fat **9g**	2	cinnamon sticks	2
Saturated fat **3g**	12	allspice berries	12
Sodium **400mg**	16	cloves	16
	24	black peppercorns	24
	2	oranges, pared rind only	2
	125 g	dried pears	4 oz
	1.5 kg	new potatoes, scrubbed and sliced	3 lb
	250 g	small carrots, halved crosswise and then quartered lengthwise	8 oz
	500 g	small leeks, sliced	1 lb
	2	sticks celery, chopped	2
	60 g	sultanas	2 oz
	1 tsp	salt	1 tsp

Put the cider in a non-reactive saucepan with the cinnamon, allspice, cloves, peppercorns and orange rind, and bring to the boil. Remove the pan from the heat, cover and leave to infuse for 30 minutes.

Add the pears to the spiced cider and set aside to soak, uncovered, for 1 hour.

Remove the pears with a slotted spoon and cut them into strips crosswise, then set them aside. Strain and reserve the soaking liquid, and discard the spices and flavourings.

Preheat the oven to 170°C (325°F or Mark 3).

Grease the bottom of a casserole. Arrange about one third of the potato slices in a layer over the bottom, then layer the carrots, pork, leeks, celery and sultanas in the casserole. Scatter the strips of pear over the top. Stir the salt into the reserved spiced cider and pour it into the casserole, then arrange the remaining potato slices on top, overlapping them slightly to make a neat lid.

Cover the casserole and cook the hotpot in the oven for 1¾ hours. Take it out of the oven and remove the lid. Tilt the casserole and spoon some liquid over the top layer of potatoes. Return the casserole to the oven, uncovered, and cook for a further 40 minutes to brown the surface.

Portuguese Pork

PORTUGUESE COOKING IS NOTED FOR ITS FREQUENT USE OF PEAS, WHICH ARE A GOOD SOURCE OF VITAMINS, PROTEIN AND FIBRE.

Serves 4
Working time: about 30 minutes
Total time: about 1 hour 15 minutes

Calories **350**
Protein **28g**
Cholesterol **70mg**
Total fat **14g**
Saturated fat **4g**
Sodium **135mg**

500 g	pork fillet, trimmed of fat, thickly sliced	1 lb
1 tbsp	safflower oil	1 tbsp
1	large onion, thinly sliced	1
2	garlic cloves, crushed	2
750 g	plum tomatoes, quartered, or 400 g (14 oz) canned tomatoes, drained	1½ lb
2 tbsp	tomato paste	2 tbsp
15 cl	dry white wine	¼ pint
15 cl	unsalted vegetable or chicken stock (recipes, page 139)	¼ pint
2 tbsp	chopped parsley	2 tbsp
2 tbsp	chopped fresh basil	2 tbsp
1 tsp	dried mixed herbs	1 tsp
½ tsp	sugar	½ tsp
⅛ tsp	salt	⅛ tsp
	freshly ground black pepper	
250 g	fresh or frozen peas	8 oz
1	sweet yellow pepper, seeded, deribbed and thinly sliced lengthwise	1

Heat the safflower oil in a heavy fireproof casserole, add the sliced onion and cook gently, stirring, until it is soft and lightly coloured — about 5 minutes. Stir in the crushed garlic, tomatoes, tomato paste, white wine and stock. Bring to the boil, stirring, then reduce the heat and add half of the chopped parsley and basil, the dried mixed herbs, sugar, salt and some freshly ground pepper. Simmer the mixture uncovered, stirring occasionally, for about 20 minutes, until the sauce is reduced and quite thick.

Meanwhile, brown the slices of pork in batches in a hot non-stick frying pan over medium-high heat, then drain them on paper towels.

Add the pork slices to the casserole, cover, reduce the heat and simmer for 25 minutes, stirring occasionally, until the meat is tender. If you are using fresh peas, add these to the casserole after the pork has been cooking for 5 minutes. Add the sliced yellow pepper after 20 minutes, together with the frozen peas, if using. Just before serving the stew, stir in the remaining chopped parsley and basil.

SUGGESTED ACCOMPANIMENTS: *brown rice; green salad.*

Pork Vindaloo

Serves 8
Working time: about 15 minutes
Total time: about 26 hours
(includes marinating)

Calories **200**
Protein **22g**
Cholesterol **70mg**
Total fat **10g**
Saturated fat **3g**
Sodium **265mg**

1 kg	lean leg or neck end of pork, trimmed and cut into small cubes	2 lb
300 g	tomatoes, roughly chopped	10 oz
1	sweet green pepper, seeded and chopped	1
1	large onion, sliced	1
3	garlic cloves, crushed	3
1 tbsp	safflower oil	1 tbsp
1 tsp	cumin seeds	1 tsp
1 tsp	yellow mustard seeds	1 tsp
1 tsp	ground cinnamon	1 tsp
1 tsp	mustard powder	1 tsp
½ tsp	ground turmeric	½ tsp
10	black peppercorns, crushed	10
6	small red chili peppers, fresh or dried (caution, page 36)	6
6 tbsp	vinegar	6 tbsp
2 tbsp	plain low-fat yogurt	2 tbsp
½	lemon, grated rind and juice	½
¼ tsp	salt (optional)	¼ tsp
4 tbsp	chopped fresh coriander	4 tbsp

Heap the pork and all the other ingredients except the salt and fresh coriander in a large non-reactive bowl and mix them together well. Cover the bowl and leave to marinate for 24 hours.

Transfer the mixture to a large saucepan and simmer gently for 1½ hours, stirring occasionally and adding a little water if it appears too dry. At the end of cooking, taste a little of the stew and add the salt if required. Stir in the chopped coriander before serving.

SUGGESTED ACCOMPANIMENT: *cinnamon creamed potatoes.*

EDITOR'S NOTE: *This dish will taste even better if kept in the refrigerator and eaten the following day.*

Red Pork

Serves 4
Working time: about 25 minutes
Total time: about 1 hour and 25 minutes
(includes marinating)

Calories **235**
Protein **22g**
Cholesterol **70mg**
Total fat **15g**
Saturated fat **4g**
Sodium **180mg**

500 g	neck end of pork, trimmed of fat and cut into small cubes	1 lb
1	lemon, juice only	1
2 tbsp	safflower oil	2 tbsp
1	onion, very finely chopped	1
3	garlic cloves, crushed	3
6	large red tomatoes, finely chopped	6
1 tbsp	tomato paste	1 tbsp
1 tsp	ground turmeric	1 tsp
8	black peppercorns, crushed	8
¼ tsp	coriander seeds, crushed	¼ tsp
¼ tsp	salt	¼ tsp
8	fresh coriander sprigs, chopped	8

Put the pork into a shallow non-reactive dish with the lemon juice and leave to marinate for 1 hour.

Heat the oil in a frying pan and add the onion, garlic, tomatoes and tomato paste. Cook for 3 minutes, then add the turmeric, peppercorns and pork. Cook, uncovered, for a further 3 minutes to brown the pork; to prevent burning, you may need to add about 3 tablespoons of water. Add the coriander seeds and salt, cover the pan and cook over medium heat for a further 15 minutes, until the meat is tender.

Serve in a warmed dish garnished with the chopped fresh coriander.

SUGGESTED ACCOMPANIMENT: *a dressed salad of endive and orange segments, topped with chives and orange rind.*

Pork Dopiaza

DOPIAZA, THE INDIAN TITLE OF THIS DISH, INDICATES THAT IT
CONTAINS TWICE THE AMOUNT OF ONIONS AS MEAT.

Serves 6
Working time: about 25 minutes
Total time: about 1 hour and 15 minutes

Calories **290**
Protein **27g**
Cholesterol **80mg**
Total fat **12g**
Saturated fat **4g**
Sodium **250mg**

750 g	lean leg or neck end of pork, trimmed of fat and cut into small cubes	1½ lb
3 tbsp	safflower oil	3 tbsp
1.5 kg	onions, 1 kg (2 lb) finely sliced, 500 g (1 lb) coarsely chopped	3 lb
300 g	tomatoes, chopped	10 oz
4	garlic cloves, crushed	4
1 tsp	ground coriander	1 tsp
1 tsp	chili powder	1 tsp
1 tsp	ground cinnamon	1 tsp
4	bay leaves	4
	ground turmeric	
5 cm	piece fresh ginger root, peeled and sliced	2 inch
8	black peppercorns, crushed	8
1 tbsp	plain low-fat yogurt	1 tbsp
½ tsp	salt	½ tsp
1	lemon, juice only	1
6	fresh coriander sprigs, torn into pieces	6

Heat half of the oil in a large frying pan and add the
pork, half the sliced onions, the tomatoes, garlic,
ground coriander, chili powder, cinnamon, bay leaves
and about ½ teaspoon of turmeric. Toss the contents
of the pan and cook for 2 minutes, stirring occasionally. Add the remaining sliced onions, cover the
pan and cook gently for 1 hour or until tender.

About 15 minutes before serving, heat the remaining oil in another frying pan and add the chopped
onions, ginger, peppercorns and a pinch of turmeric
for colour. Cook until the onions are nearly golden,
then stir in the yogurt. Transfer the onions to the pork
in the first pan and add the salt and lemon juice. Serve
in the pan, garnished with the fresh coriander.

SUGGESTED ACCOMPANIMENT: *plain boiled rice.*

Vinegar Pork with Garlic

Serves 6
Working time: about 20 minutes
Total time: about 1 hour and 40 minutes
(includes marinating)

Calories **300**
Protein **33g**
Cholesterol **80mg**
Total fat **13g**
Saturated fat **5g**
Sodium **130mg**

1 kg	boned leg of pork, trimmed of fat and cut into 4 cm (1½ inch) cubes	2 lb
3 tbsp	low-sodium soy sauce or shoyu	3 tbsp
5 tbsp	distilled malt, rice or other clear vinegar	5 tbsp
2 tbsp	safflower oil	2 tbsp
1	head of garlic (about 12 cloves), cloves peeled and quartered	1
1 tsp	black peppercorns, coarsely crushed	1 tsp
350 g	waxy potatoes, quartered	12 oz

Sprinkle the meat with the soy sauce and vinegar, and leave to marinate for at least 30 minutes.

Heat the oil in a large fireproof casserole over high heat. Add the garlic and stir for a few seconds, then reduce the heat and spoon in the meat, reserving the marinade. Turn the meat for 2 to 3 minutes, until it has lost its raw look — do not let it brown. Add the peppercorns, marinade, potatoes and enough water to cover. Bring to the boil, cover and simmer for 30 minutes.

Remove the lid and increase the heat. Continue cooking for 20 to 30 minutes, stirring often, until the meat is tender and coated with a thick, syrupy sauce.

SUGGESTED ACCOMPANIMENTS: *boiled rice or sweet potatoes; sautéed okra.*

Pork Schpundra

IN THIS LIGHT ADAPTATION OF SCHPUNDRA, AN EASTERN-EUROPEAN
CASSEROLE WITH PLENTY OF BEETROOT, THE TRADITIONAL LIQUOR
KNOWN AS KVASS IS REPLACED WITH BEER, YOGURT AND MINT.

Serves 4
Working time: about 20 minutes
Total time: about 1 hour and 20 minutes

Calories **240**
Protein **25g**
Cholesterol **70mg**
Total fat **8g**
Saturated fat **3g**
Sodium **400mg**

500 g	neck end or other lean stewing pork, trimmed of fat and cut into 2 cm (¾ inch) cubes	1 lb
1 tbsp	safflower oil	1 tbsp
500 g	fresh beetroot, cut into 2 cm (¾ inch) cubes	1 lb
1	red onion, sliced	1
30 cl	light beer	½ pint
2 tbsp	barley malt syrup	2 tbsp
8	black peppercorns	8
4	allspice berries	4
1	fresh or dried bay leaf	1
1	fresh mint sprig	1
½ tsp	salt	½ tsp
1 tbsp	potato flour, dissolved in 2 tbsp water	1 tbsp
125 g	smetana or thick Greek yogurt	4 oz

Heat the oil in a large fireproof casserole. Add the
meat and brown the cubes evenly on all sides over
high heat — about 1 minute. Add the beetroot, onion,
beer, malt syrup, peppercorns, allspice, bay leaf, mint
and salt. Bring to the boil and simmer gently for 1 to
1¼ hours, until the meat is tender.

   Add the potato flour mixture to the casserole and
cook a little further to thicken the liquid, stirring all the
time. Serve hot, topping each serving with a swirl of
the smetana or yogurt.

SUGGESTED ACCOMPANIMENT: *rye bread.*

Mexican Pork

Serves 4
Working time: about 20 minutes
Total time: about 8 hours (includes soaking)

Calories **250**			
Protein **25g**	500 g	pork fillet, trimmed of fat and cut into 2.5 cm (1 inch) cubes	1 lb
Cholesterol **80mg**	60 g	dried kidney beans, soaked in cold water for 7 to 8 hours or overnight	2 oz
Total fat **11g**	1 tbsp	virgin olive oil	1 tbsp
Saturated fat **4g**	1	onion, finely chopped	1
Sodium **290mg**	1	garlic clove, crushed	1
	1 tsp	chili powder	1 tsp
	¼ tsp	ground allspice	¼ tsp
	1½ tbsp	tomato paste	1½ tbsp
	30 cl	unsalted chicken stock (recipe, page 139)	½ pint
	2 tsp	arrowroot	2 tsp
	½ tsp	salt	½ tsp
	2 tbsp	soured cream	2 tbsp
	2 tbsp	plain low-fat yogurt	2 tbsp

Drain the kidney beans, place them in a saucepan, cover with water and bring to the boil. Boil rapidly for at least 10 minutes, then reduce the heat, cover and simmer until tender — 25 to 30 minutes. Drain well.

Heat the oil in a large heavy saucepan; add the pork, onion and garlic and cook for 4 to 5 minutes, stirring frequently to brown the meat on all sides.

Stir in the chili powder, allspice and tomato paste; add the stock. Bring to the boil, then reduce the heat, cover and simmer for 20 minutes.

Add the cooked kidney beans to the pan. In a small bowl, mix the arrowroot with 2 tablespoons of cold water. Add the mixture to the pan and stir well, until the juices are thickened. Season with the salt.

Mix together the soured cream and yogurt. Spoon a quarter of the mixture on to each serving.

Red Pepper Pork with Mint

Serves 4
Working (and total) time: about 35 minutes

Calories **220**
Protein **24g**
Cholesterol **70mg**
Total fat **12g**
Saturated fat **3g**
Sodium **90mg**

500 g	pork fillet or loin, trimmed of fat and thinly sliced	1 lb
1 tbsp	virgin olive oil	1 tbsp
2	sweet red peppers, seeded, deribbed and thinly sliced	2
	freshly ground black pepper	
500 g	tomatoes, skinned, seeded and chopped	1 lb
¼ tsp	salt	¼ tsp
2 tbsp	finely chopped fresh mint	2 tbsp
45 g	fromage frais (optional)	1½ oz

Heat the oil in a heavy frying pan; add the red peppers and sauté for 1 minute. Add the pork slices and brown them over high heat. Season with some black pepper, then cover the pan and reduce the heat to low. After 5 minutes, add the tomatoes; continue to cook, covered, for 10 to 15 minutes, or until the meat is tender and the tomato-pepper mixture is well reduced. Season with the salt and some more pepper, if required.

Remove the pan from the heat and leave it to cool for 1 minute, then stir in the mint and, if you are using it, the *fromage frais*. Serve at once.

SUGGESTED ACCOMPANIMENTS: *rice, pasta or new potatoes; crusty bread; green salad.*

Fillet in Red Wine with Prunes

Serves 4
Working time: about 20 minutes
Total time: about 1 hour and 20 minutes

Calories **215**
Protein **23g**
Cholesterol **70mg**
Total fat **12g**
Saturated fat **4g**
Sodium **280mg**

500 g	pork fillet, trimmed of fat and cut crosswise into 1 cm (½ inch) thick slices	1 lb
1 tbsp	virgin olive oil	1 tbsp
1	onion, sliced	1
250 g	button mushrooms, quartered if large	8 oz
35 cl	Beaujolais or other fruity red wine	12 fl oz
8	large ready-to-eat prunes	8
1	bay leaf	1
½ tsp	salt	½ tsp
	freshly ground black pepper	
1 tsp	cornflour mixed with 1 tbsp water	1 tsp
75 g	fromage frais	2½ oz

Preheat the oven to 180°C (350°F or Mark 4).

Heat half of the oil in a heavy or non-stick frying pan and brown the slices of pork over high heat for 1 to 2 minutes on each side. As the slices are browned, transfer them to a casserole.

Add the remaining oil to the pan and reduce the heat to medium high. Add the onion and mushrooms and cook, stirring, until browned — about 5 minutes. Transfer the vegetables to the casserole.

Pour the wine into the frying pan and bring it to the boil, stirring to mix in any sediment on the bottom of the pan. Transfer the wine to the casserole and add the prunes, bay leaf, salt and some pepper. Cover the casserole tightly and cook in the oven for 1 hour.

Using a slotted spoon, transfer the pork, prunes and vegetables to a heated serving dish; keep hot in a low oven. Discard the bay leaf. Pour the cooking liquid into a saucepan; add the cornflour mixture to the pan, stirring well. Bring to the boil, stirring until the sauce is smooth and thickened. Remove the pan from the heat and stir in the *fromage frais*.

Pour the sauce over the pork and mix in gently. Serve immediately.

EDITOR'S NOTE: *The prunes used in this recipe are sold for eating straight from the packet, and do not require presoaking or stoning. If you use ordinary dried prunes, soak them in cold water for 3 hours and stone them before cooking.*

Coachman's Pork

IN THIS ADAPTATION OF A TRADITIONAL SCANDINAVIAN DISH,
THE MEAT AND ONIONS ARE BROWNED IN A LITTLE LIGHT OIL
INSTEAD OF IN BUTTER.

Serves 6
Working time: about 40 minutes
Total time: about 2 hours and 40 minutes

Calories **235**
Protein **19g**
Cholesterol **125mg**
Total fat **7g**
Saturated fat **3g**
Sodium **280mg**

500 g	pork loin or other lean pork, cut into 1 cm (½ inch) strips	1 lb
2 tsp	safflower oil	2 tsp
750 g	onions, thickly sliced	1½ lb
4	lamb's kidneys, quartered and trimmed	4
1 kg	potatoes, cut into 3 mm (⅛ inch) slices	2 lb
17.5 cl	lager	6 fl oz
30 cl	unsalted veal stock (recipe, page 139)	½ pint
½ tsp	salt	½ tsp
	freshly ground black pepper	

Heat the oil in a large frying pan. Add the onions and cook over medium heat, stirring from time to time, until the onions start turning brown at the edges. Remove them from the pan and set aside.

In the same pan, fry the pork strips, a few at a time, until well browned. Set them aside. Fry the kidney pieces in the pan to sear them.

Preheat the oven to 190°C (375°F or Mark 5). In the bottom of a deep ovenproof dish, spread a third of the onions, then a third of the potatoes, the kidneys, another third of onions, another third of potatoes, the pork, a final layer of onions, then potatoes.

Over high heat, deglaze the frying pan with the lager. Boil rapidly until almost completely reduced, then add the stock, salt and some pepper, and bring back to the boil. Pour the liquid over the ingredients in the dish. Cover with foil and bake for 2 hours. Remove the foil after 1 hour, so the top can brown. Serve hot.

SUGGESTED ACCOMPANIMENT: *steamed winter greens.*

Fillet with Rice and Vegetables

THIS MILD VERSION OF JAMBALAYA, A SPICED RICE DISH FROM THE SOUTHERN UNITED STATES, PROVIDES AN APPETIZING FAMILY MEAL.

Serves 4
Working time: about 30 minutes
Total time: about 1 hour and 20 minutes

Calories **565**
Protein **34g**
Cholesterol **70mg**
Total fat **15g**
Saturated fat **4g**
Sodium **330mg**

500 g	pork fillet, trimmed of fat and cubed	1 lb
2 tbsp	safflower oil	2 tbsp
1	onion, chopped	1
1	large garlic clove, finely chopped	1
500 g	ripe tomatoes, skinned and chopped	1 lb
45 cl	puréed tomatoes	¾ pint
1 tsp	mild chili powder	1 tsp
1 tbsp	Worcester sauce	1 tbsp
	cayenne pepper	
½ tsp	salt	½ tsp
	freshly ground black pepper	
	Tabasco sauce	
1	sweet green pepper, seeded, deribbed and diced	1
2	sticks celery, diced	2
1	aubergine (about 250 g/8 oz), cubed	1
250 g	courgettes, cubed	8 oz
250 g	long-grain rice	8 oz

Heat 1 tablespoon of the oil in a large fireproof casserole over high heat. Add the pork cubes and cook until the meat is sealed — about 2 minutes — stirring all the time. Stir in the onion and garlic, and cook for a further minute.

Add the chopped tomatoes, puréed tomatoes, chili powder, Worcester sauce, a pinch of cayenne, the salt, some black pepper and a few drops of Tabasco sauce, and stir well. Cover and cook gently for 20 minutes, stirring from time to time.

Meanwhile, heat the remaining oil in a frying pan over moderate heat. Add the green pepper, celery and aubergine, and cook gently for 5 minutes, then stir in the courgettes and cook for a further 5 minutes.

Add the rice and vegetables to the meat in the casserole. Cover again and continue cooking for 10 to 15 minutes, or until the rice is tender and all the excess liquid has been absorbed. Depending on how much liquid the vegetables exude, you may need to add a little water from time to time. Fluff up the rice with a fork and serve hot.

SUGGESTED ACCOMPANIMENT: *tossed green salad.*

Blanquette Anisette

IN THIS ADAPTATION OF A TRADITIONAL BLANQUETTE — A STEW
IN A WHITE SAUCE USUALLY MADE WITH VEAL — SKIMMED MILK AND
SMETANA TAKE THE PLACE OF EGGS AND CREAM. THE FENNEL
AND SPIRIT COMBINED GIVE THE DISTINCTIVE FLAVOUR OF ANISE.

Serves 4
Working time: about 40 minutes
Total time: about 1 hour and 40 minutes

Calories **250**
Protein **25g**
Cholesterol **100mg**
Total fat **8g**
Saturated fat **3g**
Sodium **370mg**

500 g	neck end, blade or other stewing pork, trimmed of fat and cut into cubes	1 lb
¾ litre	unsalted chicken stock (recipe, page 139) or water	1¼ pints
1	fennel bulb, feathery top reserved	1
1	clove (optional)	1
1	bay leaf, fresh or dried	1
3	shallots, peeled and separated (optional)	3
100 g	white button mushrooms	3½ oz
15 cl	dry white wine	¼ pint
1 to 2 tbsp	fresh lemon juice	1 to 2 tbsp
200 g	white baby turnips, or larger turnips, halved or quartered	7 oz
½ tsp	salt	½ tsp
15 cl	skimmed milk	¼ pint
½ tsp	potato flour	½ tsp
1	egg yolk	1
4 tbsp	smetana	4 tbsp
1 tbsp	anise-flavoured spirit (optional)	1 tbsp

Put the pork in a large casserole and add the stock or water to cover. Bring to the boil slowly and skim the surface before adding the fennel bulb — studded with the clove, if you are using it — the bay leaf and, if you are using them, the shallots.

Simmer very gently, skimming occasionally, for 1 hour or until the meat is nearly tender. Cook the mushrooms for a minute or two in the white wine, with a dash of lemon juice added to preserve their whiteness. Add the mushrooms to the casserole together with their cooking liquid, then add the turnips and salt. Simmer for a further 20 minutes.

Test the vegetables for tenderness and drain the contents of the casserole, reserving the cooking liquid. Discard the bay leaf, clove and the shallots, if used. Cut the fennel bulb into quarters, or pieces of similar size to the other vegetables.

Strain the cooking liquid through a fine sieve into a measuring jug. Reserve 1 tablespoon of the milk, and add the remaining milk to the cooking liquid to make up ½ litre (16 fl oz). Combine the potato flour with the reserved tablespoon of milk, and beat together with the egg yolk and smetana. Beat a little of the stock-and-milk liquid into the egg liaison, then whisk the liaison into the rest of the stock; return the stock to the casserole and bring gently to simmering point, stirring or whisking all the time.

Return the pork and vegetables to the casserole and continue simmering very gently until the liquid coats the back of a spoon; do not allow it to boil, or it may curdle. Remove from the heat, stir in the spirit, if using, and add lemon juice to taste. Finely chop the fennel tops and scatter this over the top before serving.

Frikadeller Pork

FRIKADELLER ARE SCANDINAVIAN MEATBALLS MADE WITH LEAN
PORK AND VEAL. IN THIS RECIPE, THE AMOUNT OF CALORIES
PER PORTION IS KEPT VERY LOW BY COMBINING THE MEAT WITH
FRESH VEGETABLES.

Serves 8
Working (and total) time: about 1 hour

Calories **112**
Protein **17g**
Cholesterol **62mg**
Total fat **4g**
Saturated fat **3g**
Sodium **206mg**

350 g	neck end or other lean pork	12 oz
350 g	lean veal topside	12 oz
1½ tbsp	potato flour	1½ tbsp
20 cl	soda water, or 1 tsp bicarbonate of soda dissolved in water	7 fl oz
1	onion, finely chopped	1
1½ tsp	ground caraway seeds	1½ tsp
¾ tsp	salt	¾ tsp
1½ tbsp	kummel (optional)	1½ tbsp
250 g	broccoli florets	8 oz
250 g	cauliflower florets	8 oz
250 g	small carrots	8 oz
250 g	kohlrabi or turnips	8 oz
1.5 litres	unsalted vegetable stock (recipe, page 139)	2½ pints
1	small bunch parsley or carrot tops, finely chopped	1

Mince both the pork and veal in a food processor until
a smooth amalgam is formed; or put the meats
through a mincer three times. Beat the potato flour and
soda water into the meat until the mixture is almost
fluffy in appearance; mix in the onion, caraway seeds,
salt and the kummel, if you are using it. Leave the
mixture to chill in the refrigerator.

Cut the vegetables into approximately equal-sized
pieces, about 2.5 cm (1 inch) across; leave the root
vegetables whole if they are sufficiently young and
small. Divide the stock between two wide cooking pots
and bring both liquids to the boil.

To cook the frikadeller, drop teaspoons of the meat
mixture into one pot of simmering stock. You will have
at least three dozen little dumplings and, as they ex-
pand considerably during cooking, it will be necessary
to poach them in batches. Poach each batch at a
gentle simmer for 5 to 7 minutes, turning occasionally
with a slotted spoon (the frikadeller are not necessarily
cooked through when they rise to the surface of the
liquid). Replenish the liquid in the pan with hot water
as the cooking stock evaporates. Remove each batch
of cooked frikadeller with a slotted spoon and keep
warm in a colander placed on the second cooking pot.

While poaching the last batch of frikadeller, cook the
vegetables in the second pot of simmering stock.
Drain them when they are done — they should retain
some bite — and reserve the stock.

Once all the frikadeller and the vegetables are
cooked, combine the cooking liquids and strain
through a fine-meshed sieve into a fireproof casserole
or one of the cooking pots already used. Return the
liquid to simmering point and add all the frikadeller and
vegetables. Warm through briefly and scatter with the
chopped parsley or carrot tops before serving.

Wine and Vegetable Pork

Serves 4
Working time: about 30 minutes
Total time: about 45 minutes

Calories **300**
Protein **24g**
Cholesterol **75mg**
Total fat **15g**
Saturated fat **5g**
Sodium **310mg**

500 g	pork fillet, trimmed of fat and cut into 4 cm (1½ inch) strips	1 lb
	freshly ground black pepper	
2 tbsp	virgin olive oil	2 tbsp
1	large onion, chopped	1
2	carrots, sliced into rounds	2
1	leek, white part only, sliced into rounds	1
30 cl	white wine	½ pint
10 cl	unsalted vegetable stock (recipe, page 139)	3½ fl oz
1 tbsp	finely chopped fresh thyme, or 1 tsp dried thyme	1 tbsp
1 tbsp	finely chopped fresh rosemary, or 1 tsp dried rosemary	1 tbsp
1	bay leaf	1
250 g	tomatoes	8 oz
250 g	mange-tout, strings removed	8 oz
1 tbsp	single cream (optional)	1 tbsp
½ tsp	salt	½ tsp
4 tbsp	chopped parsley	4 tbsp

Grind a little black pepper over the pork strips and rub it in with the tips of your fingers. Heat the oil in a non-stick fireproof casserole over high heat until it is smoking, then add the pork, stirring vigorously. When the meat is browned on both sides — about 2 minutes — remove it and keep it warm.

Reduce the heat and add the onion, carrots and leek to the casserole. Cook gently until the vegetables soften — about 3 minutes. Add the wine, stock, thyme, rosemary and bay leaf, and bring to the boil. Simmer for 10 minutes, stirring occasionally.

Meanwhile, core the tomatoes and cut a small cross in the skin on the bottom of each, then plunge them into boiling water for 10 to 12 seconds. Remove the tomatoes and refresh them in cold water. Peel off the skin in sections, starting at the bottom of each tomato and working towards the stem end; press out the seeds and cut the tomatoes into slivers. Put the mange-tout in a pan of boiling water and cook until they are softened but still crunchy — about 3 minutes. Drain and refresh under cold running water.

Return the meat to the casserole along with any juices that have collected in the dish, and cook gently for 5 minutes. Add the cream, if you are using it, and the salt, and stir. After 1 minute, add the mange-tout, tomatoes and 3 tablespoons of the parsley, and warm through quickly. Transfer the contents of the pan to a warmed serving dish, sprinkle with the remaining parsley and serve immediately.

SUGGESTED ACCOMPANIMENT: *plain boiled rice.*

EDITOR'S NOTE: *Instead of mange-tout, 175 g (6 oz) of topped and tailed French beans may be used in this recipe.*

Fillet with Wheat Grains and Gin

Serves 4
Working time: about 20 minutes
Total time: about 10 hours (includes soaking)

Calories **280**
Protein **24g**
Cholesterol **60mg**
Total fat **8g**
Saturated fat **3g**
Sodium **75mg**

350 g	pork fillet, cut into strips about 6 by 1 cm (2½ by ½ inch)	12 oz
100 g	whole wheat grains	3½ oz
1	orange, peeled and divided into segments, 1 strip of rind pared and reserved	1
10	juniper berries, crushed	10
17.5 cl	fresh orange juice	6 fl oz
3 tbsp	dry gin	3 tbsp
60 g	spring onions, thinly sliced	2 oz
45 g	fromage frais	1½ oz
1 tbsp	chopped parsley	1 tbsp
	freshly ground black pepper	

Place the wheat grains and the orange rind in a saucepan of cold water and leave to soak overnight.

Drain the wheat grains, add them to a saucepan of boiling water and simmer for 35 to 45 minutes, or until the grains are cooked but still have bite.

While the wheat is cooking, heat the juniper berries in a small, heavy-bottomed saucepan for about 3 minutes, then add the orange juice and gin. Warm through gently, then cover, remove from the heat and leave to infuse for 30 minutes.

Heat the juniper infusion to just below simmering point. Add the pork in two or three batches and poach each batch for 2 minutes; when cooked, lift each batch from the liquid with a slotted spoon and keep it warm. Add the spring onions to the liquid, then simmer until the liquid is reduced by one third and the spring onions are cooked. Add any juices from the pork towards the end of the cooking time. Reduce the heat to very low and whisk in the *fromage frais*.

When the wheat is cooked, drain it and place it in a warmed serving bowl, discarding the orange rind.

Remove the sauce from the heat, add the pork and parsley, and season with some black pepper. Pour the sauce and pork over the wheat grains and toss lightly with the orange segments.

Fennel Pork

Serves 6
Working (and total) time: about 40 minutes

Calories **160**			
Protein **22g**	6	boneless pork steaks (about 125 g/4 oz each), trimmed of fat	6
Cholesterol **70mg**		freshly ground black pepper	
Total fat **7g**	300 g	fennel bulbs, feathery tops reserved	10 oz
Saturated fat **3g**	35 cl	unsalted veal or chicken stock (recipes, page 139)	12 fl oz
Sodium **220mg**	1 tbsp	anise-flavoured spirit	1 tbsp
	45 g	fromage frais	1½ oz
	¼ tsp	salt	¼ tsp
		white pepper	

Using a small, sharp knife, cut into the side of each steak to make a deep cavity (page 12, Step 3). Season the pockets with some freshly ground black pepper.

Remove three outer leaves from each fennel bulb, and cut each leaf in half. In a large pan simmer the leaves in the stock for 5 minutes. Lift them from the stock with a slotted spoon and divide them among the cavities in the chops. Place the chops in a steamer.

Chop the remaining fennel and add it to the stock. Place the steamer over the stock and steam the steaks for 6 to 8 minutes, turning them over half way through. Remove the steamer from the pan and keep the steaks warm.

Continue to boil the fennel in the stock until it is tender — about 5 minutes — then remove it with a slotted spoon and set aside. Add the spirit to the stock and boil until the liquid has reduced to about 4 tablespoons, then put it in a food processor with the fennel and *fromage frais*, and purée them. Transfer the purée to a pan, add the salt and some white pepper, and warm over low heat, stirring occasionally.

Place the steaks on a warmed dish, spoon the sauce round them, and garnish with the fennel fronds.

SUGGESTED ACCOMPANIMENT: *green beans.*

Pork Couscous

Serves 6
Working time: about 30 minutes
Total time: about 1 hour and 30 minutes
(includes marinating)

Calories **400**
Protein **25g**
Cholesterol **80mg**
Total fat **15g**
Saturated fat **5g**
Sodium **380mg**

750 g	neck end or other lean pork, trimmed of fat and cut into 1 cm (½ inch) cubes	1½ lb
1	onion	1
1	lemon, juice only	1
1 tsp	salt	1 tsp
½ tsp	ground cinnamon	½ tsp
5 cm	piece fresh ginger root	2 inch
6	small turnips, or chunks of large turnips	6
6	small carrots, or chunks of large carrots	6
350 g	aubergines cut into 2.5 cm (1 inch) cubes	12 oz
300 g	small courgettes, sliced diagonally	10 oz
6	fresh dates, stoned and halved	6
125 g	cooked chick-peas	4 oz
500 g	couscous	1 lb
1½ tbsp	harissa	1½ tbsp

Purée the onion with the lemon juice, salt and cinnamon in a food processor; or grate the onion finely, then mix it with the other three ingredients. Marinate the pork in this paste for 30 minutes.

Place the ginger in about 60 cl (1 pint) of water in a saucepan over which you can fit a closely fitting two-tier steamer with a lid. Bring the water to the boil.

Pick out the pieces of meat from the marinade, but do not scrape off any of the paste that sticks to them. Arrange the meat in the bottom tier of the steamer together with the turnips, carrots and aubergines. Set this, covered, over the boiling water and let it steam for 30 minutes. Check from time to time that the water has not boiled away.

Add the courgettes, dates and chick-peas to the meat mixture. Cover and steam for 20 minutes more.

Meanwhile, put the couscous in a large bowl. Pour on 45 cl (¾ pint) of lukewarm water and leave the couscous to swell for 10 minutes, stirring occasionally to prevent lumps from forming.

About 10 minutes before the meat and vegetables are ready, put the couscous in the upper tier of the steamer to heat through uncovered. The couscous is done when the steam begins to penetrate its surface. If this has not happened by the time the meat and vegetables are cooked, take out the bottom tier and put the couscous directly over the saucepan.

Pile the couscous on to a serving platter. Arrange the meat and vegetables on top. Dilute the harissa with 30 cl (½ pint) of the gingery steaming liquid, and serve it separately. The remaining liquid may also be passed round to moisten the meat and vegetables.

Pork and Burghul Meatballs

Serves 6
Working time: about 30 minutes
Total time: about 1 hour and 10 minutes

Calories **240**
Protein **27g**
Cholesterol **70mg**
Total fat **9g**
Saturated fat **5g**
Sodium **230mg**

350 g	neck end or other lean pork, minced	12 oz
90 g	fine-grade burghul	3 oz
3 tbsp	very finely chopped onion	3 tbsp
¾ tsp	ground roasted cumin seed	¾ tsp
½ tsp	salt	½ tsp
	freshly ground black pepper	
4 tbsp	finely chopped parsley	4 tbsp
125 g	thick Greek yogurt	4 oz
1 tsp	arrowroot	1 tsp
1	garlic clove, finely chopped	1
½ tsp	grated lemon rind	½ tsp
	cayenne pepper	

Knead the minced pork with the burghul, onion, cumin,

salt and some pepper. Let the mixture stand for 10 minutes, knead again briefly, then form into 24 balls. Roll the balls in the parsley, pressing them in so that the herb coating sticks. Arrange the balls, in a single layer, in a steamer over a saucepan of boiling water, cover and steam for 40 minutes.

Towards the end of this time, put the yogurt in a small pan. Mix the arrowroot with a little cold water, and stir into the yogurt; add the garlic, the lemon rind and a pinch of cayenne. Gradually beat in 6 tablespoons of hot water from the steaming pan and bring to the boil over medium heat, stirring constantly. When the sauce has thickened, let it sit for 5 minutes off the heat, so that the arrowroot is completely absorbed.

Bring the sauce back to the boil just before serving. Serve the meatballs directly from the steamer, accompanied by the hot sauce.

SUGGESTED ACCOMPANIMENT: *rice mixed with peas.*

EDITOR'S NOTE: *A bamboo steamer will provide a wider and flatter surface for the meatballs than an ordinary steamer.*

3 *Thinly sliced pork, mushrooms, daikon radish, prawns and other ingredients stand ready to be folded inside moistened rice-paper wrappers (recipe, page 102).*

Dishes with an Unusual Twist

No meat is more versatile than pork, and the recipes in this chapter offer many variations on the basic cooking methods encompassed in the previous two. The diverse collection of dishes that follows demonstrates that the need to control fat levels and calories can be a spur to invention rather than a handicap.

Some of the recipes are devised for serving cold. Such dishes as pork and spinach terrine *(page 101)*, pork salad with mustard vinaigrette *(page 118)* and stuffed pig's trotters *(page 117)* derive their inspiration from the French charcuterie, or cooked pork shop. Traditional charcuterie dishes were a means of using up the pig's abundant fat which, unlike that of beef and lamb, is very palatable when eaten cold. But the charcuterie recipes in this chapter are prepared with ingredients and cooking techniques that keep the fat level within reasonable bounds.

Other recipes in the chapter extend the meat with a satisfying complement of pastry, potatoes, bread, beans or rice. An international selection of rice dishes includes an Italian risotto flavoured with Parmesan cheese *(page 106)*, a Turkish pilaff with pine-nuts and currants *(page 107)* and a Dutch-Indonesian *nasi goreng (page 104)*, where prawns and omelette slices complement the pork.

A further group of recipes feature pork presented in edible wrappers. Pork stuffings are enclosed in ravioli *(page 112)*, cannelloni *(page 120)*, phyllo pastry *(page 119)*, Chinese cabbage leaves *(page 103)* and rice-paper wrappers *(opposite)*. Conversely, thin slices of lean pork are themselves used as receptacles for a vegetable filling *(page 109)*.

The recipes for stuffings and meatballs in this chapter frequently call for lean minced pork. To avoid the excessive fat content of the minced pork habitually offered for sale, you can either order lean mince specially from your butcher or buy a lean cut of pork and mince it yourself. The technique for mincing meat by hand is demonstrated on page 11.

Ham with Broad Beans

Serves 6
Working time: about 15 minutes
Total time: about 30 minutes

Calories **130**
Protein **10g**
Cholesterol **15mg**
Total fat **4g**
Saturated fat **2g**
Sodium **390mg**

175 g	lean ham, diced	6 oz
750 g	shelled broad beans	1½ lb
1 tsp	safflower oil	1 tsp
1 tbsp	plain flour	1 tbsp
4 tbsp	white wine (optional)	4 tbsp
	freshly ground black pepper	
2 tbsp	single cream	2 tbsp
2 tbsp	finely chopped fresh summer savory, or 1 ½ tsp dried summer savory	2 tbsp

Bring a saucepan of water to the boil, add the broad beans and simmer until they are soft but still resistant — about 5 minutes. Strain them and set aside, reserving the cooking liquid.

Heat the oil in a large heavy-bottomed saucepan; add the diced ham and fry gently for 1 minute. Stir in the flour and cook for a further minute, stirring continuously. Add the wine, if you are using it, and about 15 cl (¼ pint) of the bean cooking liquid. Simmer the mixture for 2 minutes, adding more cooking liquid if the sauce is too thick. Season with some freshly ground black pepper. Add the cream and allow the liquid to bubble up once.

Stir the beans into the pan, warm through, sprinkle with the summer savory and serve.

EDITOR'S NOTE: *The skin of broad beans is rich in fibre but has a slightly bitter taste; if preferred, the beans may be peeled before they are cooked.*

Pork and Spinach Terrine

Serves 12
Working time: about 45 minutes
Total time: about 11 hours (includes chilling)

Calories **135**
Protein **16g**
Cholesterol **45mg**
Total fat **5g**
Saturated fat **2g**
Sodium **190mg**

750 g	lean pork steaks, trimmed of fat	1½ lb
1	large onion, finely chopped	1
125 g	fresh wholemeal breadcrumbs	4 oz
2	garlic cloves, crushed	2
1	egg, beaten	1
1 tbsp	virgin olive oil	1 tbsp
1½ tsp	chopped fresh sage	1½ tsp
½ tsp	salt	½ tsp
	freshly ground black pepper	
150 g	boneless chicken breast, skinned	5 oz
1 tbsp	dry vermouth	1 tbsp
12	large spinach leaves, washed and stems trimmed	12
	lemon slices, for garnish	

Mince the pork in a food processor or by hand *(page 11)*. Put the pork into a bowl and add the onion, breadcrumbs, garlic, egg, oil, sage, half the salt and some pepper. Mix well together and set aside.

Cut the chicken breast into thin slices and place in a bowl with the dry vermouth, the remaining salt and some pepper. Reserve eight spinach leaves; finely shred the remainder, add them to the chicken and mix well. Preheat the oven to 180°C (350°F or Mark 4).

Blanch the reserved spinach leaves in a little boiling water in a saucepan for 1 minute. Drain and refresh with cold water, then drain well again. Pat the leaves dry on paper towels. Use the spinach leaves to line the base and sides of a 1 kg (2 lb) loaf tin: arrange three leaves, slightly overlapping, over the base and along each side of the tin, and place the remaining leaves at either end of the tin. Allow the edges of the leaves to overlap the rim of the tin.

Press half of the pork mixture into the lined tin. Arrange the chicken slices over the pork, then top with the remaining pork mixture and press to level the surface. Fold the overlapping spinach leaves over the mixture, then cover tightly with lightly greased foil and place the loaf tin inside a roasting tin half-filled with cold water. Cook in the oven for 1¾ hours.

Remove the loaf tin from the oven, cover it with clean foil and weight down with a heavy weight placed on a small board or lid that fits over the top of the terrine. Leave to cool, then chill in the refrigerator for about 8 hours. Turn the terrine out on to a serving board or platter. Pat it dry with paper towels, and garnish with the lemon slices. Serve sliced.

SUGGESTED ACCOMPANIMENT: *tomato, herb and onion salad; mixed green salad; granary bread.*

EDITOR'S NOTE: *Vine leaves may be used instead of spinach. If preserved in brine, they should be rinsed well to remove salt.*

Vietnamese Spring Rolls

SPRING ROLLS ARE USUALLY DEEP FRIED, WHICH ADDS
CONSIDERABLY TO THEIR CALORIE CONTENT. HERE, THE DEEP-
FRYING IS OMITTED, AND THE ROLLS RETAIN THE FRESHNESS
OF BOTH THE INGREDIENTS AND THE WRAPPERS.

Serves 4 as a main course, 8 as a starter
Working time: about 45 minutes
Total time: about 2 hours (includes chilling)

Calories **235**
Protein **26g**
Cholesterol **90mg**
Total fat **11g**
Saturated fat **3g**
Sodium **140mg**

350 g	pork fillet	12 oz
5 cm	piece fresh ginger root, peeled and sliced	2 inch
14	spring onions, white parts only	14
3 tbsp	low-sodium soy sauce or shoyu	3 tbsp
½ litre	unsalted vegetable or chicken stock (recipes, page 139)	16 fl oz
250 g	daikon radish, peeled and cut into thin 4 cm (1½ inch) strips	8 oz
1 tbsp	safflower oil	1 tbsp
1 or 2	fresh green chili peppers, finely sliced (caution, page 36)	1 or 2
100 g	peeled prawns	3½ oz
20 g	dried shiitake mushrooms, soaked in warm water for 20 minutes, drained and thinly sliced	¾ oz
90 g	bean sprouts	3 oz
16	crisp cos or iceberg lettuce leaves	16
16	rice-paper wrappers	16
45 g	fresh basil or mint leaves	1½ oz

Put the pork in a saucepan and add the ginger, two of
the spring onions, 2 tablespoons of the soy sauce and
35 cl (12 fl oz) of the stock. Bring to the boil, skim off
any froth that rises to the surface, then cover and simmer until the pork is tender — about 20 minutes.
Leave the pork to cool in the liquid — about 1 hour.

Meanwhile, cook the daikon in the remaining stock
for 1 to 2 minutes to soften it. Drain and set it aside.

To make spring onion brushes for the garnish, make

three or four 2.5 cm (1 inch) long cuts through the tops of the white stems of eight of the spring onions. Put the onions in a bowl of iced water and leave until the sliced tops have curled — about 30 minutes.

When the pork is cold, remove it from the liquid and slice it into thin strips. Finely chop the remaining spring onions. Heat the oil in a wok or deep, heavy frying pan. Throw in the chopped spring onions and chili peppers and stir-fry over moderate heat for 1 to 2 minutes to flavour the oil. Increase the heat, add the pork, daikon, prawns, mushrooms, bean sprouts and the remaining soy sauce, and stir-fry until the ingredients are thoroughly mixed and heated through — about 3 minutes. Remove from the heat.

Blanch the lettuce leaves in boiling water for 30 seconds, then remove the central vein of each leaf with a knife. Dip the rice-paper wrappers one at a time in a bowl of tepid water and gently shake off excess water.

Arrange the wrappers flat on a board and place one lettuce leaf in the centre of each wrapper. Place a few basil or mint leaves on the lettuce, then a spoonful of the filling. Roll the wrappers up round the filling, tucking in the sides as you proceed. Arrange the spring rolls on individual plates and garnish with the spring onion brushes. Serve cold.

SUGGESTED ACCOMPANIMENT: *a dipping sauce made from low-sodium soy sauce or shoyu with crushed garlic, finely chopped chili pepper and lemon juice.*

Stuffed Chinese Cabbage Leaves

Serves 6
Working (and total) time: about 1 hour

Calories **250**
Protein **27g**
Cholesterol **90mg**
Total fat **14g**
Saturated fat **5g**
Sodium **230mg**

750 g	pork fillet, trimmed of fat and minced	1½ lb
12	Chinese cabbage leaves	12
1	onion, finely chopped	1
175 g	brown cap or oyster mushrooms, chopped	6 oz
2	oranges, juice and grated rind of 1½ pared, julienned rind of the other half	2
½ tsp	salt	½ tsp
	freshly ground black pepper	
½ tsp	grated nutmeg	½ tsp
2 tbsp	safflower oil	2 tbsp
1 tbsp	low-sodium soy sauce or shoyu	1 tsbp

Blanch the cabbage leaves in boiling water for 1 minute and drain them flat on paper towels. Sweat the onion in a heavy frying pan until transparent, then add the mushrooms and stir-fry for 4 to 5 minutes.

In a bowl, mix together the pork, onion and mushrooms, and the grated orange rind; season with the salt, some pepper and the nutmeg. Pare down the thick part of the cabbage stems with a sharp knife so the leaves will wrap easily round the stuffing. Place about 1½ tablespoons of the pork mixture on the stem end of each leaf, then roll up and tuck in the sides.

Heat the oil in the frying pan and fry the parcels, seam side down, for about 7 minutes, then turn and cook for a further 7 minutes, or until golden. Remove the cooked parcels to a serving dish. Deglaze the pan with the soy sauce and the orange juice; reduce the liquid for a minute or so, and pour it over the parcels. Garnish with the julienned orange rind and serve.

Nasi Goreng

THIS VERSION OF A TRADITIONAL DUTCH INDONESIAN DISH, WHICH IS
USUALLY TOPPED WITH A FOUR-EGG OMELETTE CUT INTO SLICES, IS
GARNISHED WITH A SINGLE EGG. TO REDUCE THE CHOLESTEROL
CONTENT STILL FURTHER, THE OMELETTE MAY BE OMITTED.

Serves 6
Working time: about 25 minutes
Total time: about 1 hour and 15 minutes

Calories **350**
Protein **25g**
Cholesterol **120mg**
Total fat **12g**
Saturated fat **3g**
Sodium **125mg**

350 g	pork fillet, trimmed of fat and cut into 1 cm (½ inch) cubes	12 oz
250 g	long-grain brown rice	8 oz
2 tbsp	safflower oil	2 tbsp
1	large onion, quartered and thinly sliced	1
1	garlic clove, chopped	1
1	green chili pepper, seeded and chopped, plus a few thin rings for garnish (caution, page 36)	1
125 g	boneless chicken breast, skinned and cut into 1 cm (½ inch) cubes	4 oz
½ tsp	ground turmeric	½ tsp
½ tsp	paprika	½ tsp
¼ tsp	cayenne pepper	¼ tsp
2 tbsp	low-sodium soy sauce or shoyu	2 tbsp
1	large tomato, skinned, seeded and cut into thin slivers	1
175 g	peeled prawns, deveined	6 oz
Rolled omelette		
1	egg	1
1 tsp	low-sodium soy sauce or shoyu	1 tsp
1 tsp	safflower oil	1 tsp

Cook the brown rice in a large, covered, saucepan of boiling water until tender — about 40 minutes. Drain well, rinse under cold running water, drain well again and set aside.

Heat the oil in a large heavy frying pan. Add the sliced onion, garlic and chopped chili pepper, and cook gently for 3 minutes, stirring frequently. Stir in the pork and chicken cubes, and cook gently for 4 minutes, stirring. Add the turmeric, paprika and cayenne pepper and mix well, then stir in the drained rice and continue cooking the mixture for a further 4 minutes, stirring constantly. Add the soy sauce, tomato slivers and half of the prawns, and heat through for 2 to 3 minutes. Turn the mixture on to a warmed serving platter and keep warm while you make the omelette.

In a bowl, beat the egg with the soy sauce. Heat the oil in a heavy 15 to 17.5 cm (6 to 7 inch) diameter frying pan. Add the egg mixture and tilt the pan to cover the base evenly. Cook over gentle heat until the omelette is set — 45 seconds to 1 minute. Loosen the omelette from the pan and turn it out on to a board, then roll up the omelette and cut it into thin slices.

Arrange the omelette slices either round the base of the rice mixture or over the top. Garnish with the reserved rings of chili pepper and the remaining prawns, and serve immediately.

Pork and Salsify Pie

Serves 6
Working time: about 1 hour
Total time: about 4 hours and 15 minutes
(includes marinating)

Calories **340**
Protein **17g**
Cholesterol **65mg**
Total fat **17g**
Saturated fat **8g**
Sodium **310mg**

500 g	neck end, blade or other lean pork for stewing, trimmed of fat and cut into 2.5 cm (1 inch) pieces	1 lb
15 cl	dry white wine	¼ pint
3	garlic cloves, crushed	3
1	small onion, quartered	1
2	fresh bay leaves	2
2	fresh thyme sprigs	2
¼ tsp	salt	¼ tsp
	freshly ground black pepper	
½	lemon, juice only	½
250 g	salsify	8 oz
30 cl	unsalted vegetable stock (recipe, page 139)	½ pint
8	baby onions	8
125 g	tomatoes, skinned, seeded and chopped	4 oz
1 tbsp	capers, rinsed and chopped	1 tbsp
½ tsp	green peppercorns, drained and rinsed if bottled	½ tsp
1 tsp	arrowroot, mixed with 1 tsp stock or water	1 tsp
Pastry dough		
175 g	plain unbleached flour	6 oz
¼ tsp	salt	¼ tsp
45 g	unsalted butter, cut into small cubes	1½ oz
45 g	hard white vegetable fat, cut into small cubes	1½ oz

Place the pork in a shallow, non-reactive dish and add the wine, garlic, onion, bay leaves, thyme, salt and a little pepper. Leave to marinate for 2 hours.

To make the dough, sift the flour and salt into a large bowl. Add the butter and vegetable fat, and rub them into the flour with your fingertips until the mixture has a coarse, mealy texture. Sprinkle 1 to 2 tablespoons of water over the mixture, and stir with a knife until the dough begins to cohere. Gather the dough into a ball, pressing it with your hands, then wrap it in plastic film or greaseproof paper, and chill for 15 minutes.

Transfer the meat with its marinade to a saucepan, bring gently to the boil and skim as necessary. Simmer gently for 30 minutes.

Meanwhile, add the lemon juice to a pan of water. Scrub and peel the salsify under running water, cut it into 2.5 cm (1 inch) lengths, and plunge these immediately into the acidulated water. Cook the salsify until half-tender — about 20 minutes — then drain.

Remove the meat from its cooking liquid. Discard the onion, garlic and bay leaves, and add the stock to the cooking liquid. Return the meat to the pan, add the salsify and baby onions, and simmer for a further 30 minutes, until the meat is nearly tender.

Preheat the oven to 190°C (375°F or Mark 5). Place a funnel in the centre of a deep pie dish, then transfer the meat and vegetables from the pan to the dish with the tomatoes, capers and peppercorns. Discard the thyme sprigs. In another pan, measure out 30 cl (½ pint) of cooking liquid (adding additional stock, wine or water, if necessary). Blend in the arrowroot and bring to the boil. Simmer gently for a minute or two until slightly thickened, then pour into the pie dish.

Roll out the dough so that it will overlap the edges of the pie dish by about 2.5 cm (1 inch). Lift the dough on to the dish with the aid of a rolling pin, cutting a small slit to allow the funnel to protrude; fold the excess dough under to give a double thickness round the rim, and crimp the edges to the rim of the dish with your fingers. Bake in the oven for 40 minutes. Serve hot.

EDITOR'S NOTE: *Scorzonera may be substituted for salsify.*

Pork Risotto

Serves 4
Working time: about 25 minutes
Total time: about 40 minutes

Calories **460**
Protein **24g**
Cholesterol **55mg**
Total fat **12g**
Saturated fat **4g**
Sodium **100mg**

350 g	pork fillet, trimmed of fat and cut into small cubes	12 oz
1 tbsp	virgin olive oil	1 tbsp
1	onion, finely chopped	1
1	garlic clove, crushed	1
125 g	button mushrooms, roughly chopped	4 oz
½ tsp	chopped fresh sage	½ tsp
250 g	Italian round-grain rice	8 oz
½ tsp	salt	½ tsp
	freshly ground black pepper	
30 cl	dry white wine	½ pint
125 g	shelled peas, blanched in boiling water, or frozen peas	4 oz
1 tbsp	freshly grated Parmesan cheese	1 tbsp
3 tbsp	flat-leaf parsley, torn into small pieces	3 tbsp

Heat the olive oil in a heavy-bottomed saucepan over medium heat and brown the cubes of meat. Stir in the onion and continue cooking until the onion begins to turn golden at the edges. Add the garlic, mushrooms and sage. When the mushrooms are wilting, increase the heat, add the rice, salt and some pepper, and stir for a couple of minutes.

Mix the white wine with an equal amount of water and pour half of the liquid into the saucepan. Reduce the heat and stir while bringing the liquid to a gentle simmer. Stir the mixture frequently as the liquid is absorbed — 5 to 10 minutes.

Pour in the rest of the liquid and the peas, bring back to a simmer and stir. Cover the pan and leave to cook very slowly, stirring from time to time until the mixture is creamy but not mushy — 10 to 15 minutes. Just before serving, stir in the cheese and parsley.

SUGGESTED ACCOMPANIMENT: *tomato salad*.

Pilaff with Pig's Heart

Serves 6
Working time: about 20 minutes
Total time: about 45 minutes

Calories **565**
Protein **15g**
Cholesterol **60mg**
Total fat **15g**
Saturated fat **3g**
Sodium **175mg**

1	pig's heart (about 250 g/8 oz), trimmed of fat and finely diced	1
2 tbsp	virgin olive oil	2 tbsp
1	onion, finely chopped	1
2 tbsp	pine-nuts	2 tbsp
350 g	long-grain rice	12 oz
2 tbsp	currants	2 tbsp
¼ tsp	sugar	¼ tsp
¼ tsp	ground allspice	¼ tsp
¼ tsp	ground cinnamon	¼ tsp
½ tsp	salt	½ tsp
	freshly ground black pepper	
3 tbsp	finely chopped parsley	3 tbsp

Heat the olive oil in a heavy-bottomed saucepan over medium heat and sauté the diced heart for about 5 minutes. Add the onion and pine-nuts, and cook until both are beginning to colour. Add the rice and stir to coat well with oil, then stir in ¾ litre (1 ¼ pints) of water and all the remaining ingredients except the parsley. Bring to the boil, reduce the heat, cover and simmer for 10 minutes.

Stir in the parsley, re-cover the pan and leave the pilaff to stand, off the heat, for 15 minutes more. Mix well and serve hot or warm.

SUGGESTED ACCOMPANIMENTS: *steamed or grilled baby courgettes; grilled and skinned sweet pepper strips.*

Scandinavian Gratin

Serves 6
Working time: about 30 minutes
Total time: about 2 hours

Calories **290**
Protein **20g**
Cholesterol **85mg**
Total fat **13g**
Saturated fat **4g**
Sodium **365mg**

250 g	pork fillet or loin, trimmed of fat and cut into thin slices	8 oz
500 g	potatoes, thinly sliced	1 lb
250 g	onions, thinly sliced	8 oz
350 g	fresh herring fillets	12 oz
1 tsp	salt	1 tsp
	white pepper	
15 cl	skimmed milk	¼ pint
1	egg yolk	1
125 g	smetana	4 oz
2	parsley sprigs, finely chopped (optional)	2

Preheat the oven to 220°C (425°F or Mark 7).

Lightly grease a 1.5 to 1.75 litre (2½ to 3 pint) oven-proof gratin dish. Layer the sliced potatoes, onions, herring fillets and pork slices in the dish, beginning and ending with a layer of potatoes and seasoning each layer lightly with the salt and some pepper. Pour the skimmed milk into the dish.

Place the dish in the centre of the oven and bake the gratin for 15 minutes, then reduce the heat to 190°C (375°F or Mark 5) and bake for a further hour. Check that all the contents of the dish are tender by inserting a skewer in the centre of the dish — it should meet with no resistance.

Remove the dish from the oven and carefully pour out the thin juices into a bowl. Beat the egg yolk with the smetana, then beat a couple of spoonfuls of the hot cooking juices into the egg liaison. Whisk this liaison into the remaining juices in the bowl and return the liquid to the dish.

Return to the oven for a further 15 minutes. If the top layer of potatoes is already browned, cover the dish with aluminium foil for the first 10 minutes; if the potatoes still look a little pale at the end of the cooking time, brown briefly under a hot grill.

Cut the gratin into wedges and serve hot, garnished with the chopped parsley, if you are using it.

SUGGESTED ACCOMPANIMENT: *a colourful salad; French beans or garden peas.*

Italian "Money-Bags"

Serves 4
Working time: about 40 minutes
Total time: about 1 hour

Calories **200**
Protein **22g**
Cholesterol **60mg**
Total fat **10g**
Saturated fat **4g**
Sodium **340mg**

350 g	pork fillet, trimmed of fat	12 oz
½ tsp	salt	½ tsp
	freshly ground black pepper	
1	ear of sweetcorn, husked, or 125 g (4 oz) sweetcorn kernels	1
250 g	broccoli	8 oz
2 tsp	virgin olive oil	2 tsp
125 g	sweet red pepper, seeded, deribbed and diced	4 oz
45 g	low-fat ricotta cheese	1½ oz
2 tbsp	fresh basil leaves, torn or chopped	2 tbsp
1 tbsp	fresh oregano, chopped	1 tbsp
30 g	low-fat mozzarella	1 oz

Cut the fillet into 20 rounds and beat these out until they are almost translucent and three times their original size *(page 12, above)*. Season lightly with half of the salt and some freshly ground black pepper.

Cook the sweetcorn cob in boiling water, covered, for about 7 minutes, allow it to cool a little, then slice off the kernels with a sharp knife. Or, if using, briefly blanch the sweetcorn kernels.

Separate the broccoli to give at least 20 tiny florets; peel and thinly dice the stems. Blanch the broccoli briefly in boiling water and drain well.

Preheat the oven to 190°C (375°F or Mark 5). Brush the base and sides of a large, shallow ovenproof dish with 1 teaspoon of the oil.

Mix the broccoli, sweetcorn and sweet pepper with the ricotta and remaining salt, and add the basil and oregano. Divide this mixture equally among the 20 pieces of fillet. Gather up the edges of each piece to enclose the filling, leaving some of the vegetable stuffing exposed to view. Divide the mozzarella into 20 tiny cubes and top each "money-bag" with a single cube. Grind a little more black pepper on to each open parcel and arrange them in the ovenproof dish. Brush the remaining oil over the exposed surfaces of meat.

Bake the parcels in the centre of the oven for 15 to 20 minutes, or until the meat is cooked through and the edges are tinged brown. If you wish, brown the mozzarella a little more under a hot grill, but do not allow the pork to stiffen too much. Serve hot.

SUGGESTED ACCOMPANIMENTS: *thin-cut green and white noodles; a crisp salad with a balsamic vinegar dressing.*

Picnic Slice

Serves 10
Working time: about 35 minutes
Total time: about 3 hours (includes chilling)

Calories **290**
Protein **13g**
Cholesterol **70mg**
Total fat **15g**
Saturated fat **6g**
Sodium **275mg**

350 g	trimmed leg or neck end of pork, minced	12 oz
125 g	brown rice	4 oz
1	bunch spring onions, chopped	1
2	eggs, hard-boiled and roughly chopped	2
2 tbsp	chopped fresh tarragon	2 tbsp
2 tbsp	capers, rinsed and drained	2 tbsp
8	green olives, stoned and roughly chopped	8
50 g	anchovy fillets, rinsed and chopped	1¾
	Flaky pastry	
200 g	plain flour	7 oz
½ tsp	salt	½ tsp
60 g	unsalted butter, slightly softened	2 oz
60 g	hard white vegetable fat	2 oz

To make the pastry dough, sift the flour and salt into a mixing bowl. Mix together the butter and vegetable fat. Rub a quarter of the fat into the flour with your fingertips until the mixture resembles breadcrumbs. Add just enough iced water to make the dough cohere, and continue to work the dough until it comes cleanly from the sides of the bowl. Shape the dough into a ball, wrap it in plastic film and place it in the refrigerator to chill for 30 minutes.

On a floured board, roll the dough into a rectangle about three times as long as it is wide. With a short side towards you, dot the top two thirds of the rectangle with another quarter of the fat, fold the bottom third of the rectangle over the centre and the top third over that, and chill for 30 minutes. Roll out, dot with fat, fold and chill in the same way two more times, then roll out the dough to make the final folds cohere. Wrap the

dough in plastic film and refrigerate it until you are ready to use it.

Bring the rice to the boil in plenty of water and stir once. Cover and simmer for about 30 minutes or until cooked, then drain the rice in a sieve and rinse under cold running water. Leave the rice in the sieve to cool.

Brown the pork in a dry non-stick frying pan. Stir in the spring onions and cook for another 2 minutes.

Preheat the oven to 220°C (425°F or Mark 7). Divide the pastry dough into two pieces. Roll each piece into a thin sheet about 30 by 25 cm (12 by 10 inches) and place these on non-stick baking sheets. Spread the rice down the centre of each sheet of pastry to within 2.5 cm (1 inch) of the ends, leaving about 7.5 cm (3 inches) of bare pastry on each side of the filling. On top of the rice lay the meat mixture and the eggs, tarragon, capers, olives and anchovies; make sure that each ingredient is evenly spread over the rice.

Brush the edges of the pastry with water, then bring the side flaps up and fold one over the other. Crimp the joints along the centre seam and at both ends to seal the two rolls. Turn each roll over so that the seam is underneath and cut several slits in the pastry top to let the steam escape.

Bake the rolls until they are golden-brown — about 15 minutes — then turn down the oven to 180°C (350°F or Mark 4) and cook for another 20 minutes.

Turn out the rolls on to a wire rack to cool completely. Transport the rolls whole to the table or picnic destination; cut into thick slices to serve.

SUGGESTED ACCOMPANIMENT: *a selection of salads.*

Pitta Pork Balls

Serves 6
Working (and total) time: about 1 hour

Calories **230**
Protein **16g**
Cholesterol **30mg**
Total fat **6g**
Saturated fat **2g**
Sodium **280mg**

250 g	pork loin, trimmed of fat and minced	8 oz
125 g	burghul	4 oz
2 tsp	safflower oil	2 tsp
1	onion, very finely chopped	1
1	garlic clove, crushed	1
2 tsp	curry powder	2 tsp
½ tsp	ground coriander	½ tsp
¼ tsp	ground cinnamon	¼ tsp
¼ tsp	salt	¼ tsp
6	wholemeal pitta breads	6
8	cos lettuce leaves, wash, dried and finely shredded	8
10 cm	piece cucumber, thinly sliced	4 inch
200 g	tomatoes, thinly sliced	7 oz
Yogurt dressing		
8 cl	plain low-fat yogurt	3 fl oz
1 tbsp	chopped fresh mint	1 tbsp
1 tbsp	fresh lemon juice	1 tbsp
	cayenne pepper	

Preheat the oven to 190°C (375°F or Mark 5). In a bowl, soak the burghul in 30 cl (½ pint) of boiling water for 15 minutes to swell and absorb the liquid.

Meanwhile, heat the oil in a small saucepan. Add the onion and garlic and cook very gently for 3 minutes, stirring occasionally. Add the curry powder, coriander and cinnamon, and cook gently for 2 minutes.

Add the onion mixture, minced pork and salt to the soaked burghul and mix thoroughly. Form the mixture into 12 neat, oval-shaped cakes about 1.5 cm (¾ inch) thick and 7.5 cm (3 inches) long. Place the cakes on a lightly greased baking sheet and cook in the oven for 35 minutes, turning half way through cooking time.

Meanwhile, make the dressing. In a bowl, mix the yogurt with the mint and lemon juice, and season with some cayenne pepper. Refrigerate until required.

Warm the pitta breads under a medium grill for about 1 minute on each side. Slit each bread along one side and open it to form a pocket. Half fill each pocket with some of the shredded lettuce leaves. Spoon a little yogurt dressing into each bread and arrange two hot pork cakes on top. Fill the sides of the pittas with a little more shredded lettuce, and add some slices of cucumber and tomato to each one. Top the filling with a spoonful of the remaining dressing. Serve at once, wrapped in napkins.

Pork Ravioli

Serves 6
Working time: about 1 hour
Total time: about 2 hours

Calories **245**
Protein **18g**
Cholesterol **80mg**
Total fat **6g**
Saturated fat **2g**
Sodium **240mg**

350 g	pork fillet, trimmed of fat and minced	12 oz
7 g	dried ceps	¼ oz
15 g	sun-dried tomatoes	½ oz
30 g	lean prosciutto, finely chopped	1 oz
175 g	fromage frais	6 oz
½ tsp	salt	½ tsp
	freshly ground black pepper	
½ tsp	arrowroot	½ tsp
15 cl	unsalted vegetable stock (recipe, page 139) or water	¼ pint
1 tbsp	tomato paste	1 tbsp
2	fresh tomatoes, skinned and seeded	2
1	small bunch fresh basil	1

Pasta dough		
200 g	strong plain flour	7 oz
30 g	semolina	1 oz
1	egg	1
½	sun-dried tomato, finely chopped (optional)	½
2 tbsp	tomato paste	2 tbsp

To make the dough for the ravioli, combine the flour, semolina and egg in a food processor for 30 seconds or until fine crumbs are formed. Mix the sun-dried tomato, if using, with the tomato paste and 2 tablespoons of hot water. Switch on the processor and pour the tomato mixture through the feeder-funnel — the pasta dough should form into small lumps, but not yet one large lump. Switch the processor on again and feed through just sufficient water to enable the dough to form a single lump. Leave the dough to rest inside the processor bowl for about 30 minutes.

Soak the ceps and dried tomato separately in four times their volume of hot water (about 10 cl/3½ fl oz) for at least 20 minutes. Combine the minced pork and prosciutto, place them in a heavy, non-stick frying pan and stir over moderate heat for about 10 minutes, or until cooked through, breaking up any lumps that form. Squeeze excess moisture out of the reconstituted ceps and tomatoes; chop them and add to the meat, retaining the soaking liquids for the pasta sauce. Add a quarter of the *fromage frais* to the mixture and season lightly with the salt and some pepper. Allow the filling to cool a little before making up the ravioli.

If using a manual pasta extruder, pass the dough at least once through each successive setting on the rollers, flouring lightly whenever the dough feels sticky. You should have four lengths of fairly thin pasta dough, ready to be cut into ravioli. Alternatively, roll out the dough with a rolling pin until almost translucent, making two lengths of pasta of about the same size.

If you are using a ravioli tray or attachment, follow the manufacturer's instructions; otherwise simply spoon small piles of the mixture (about 2 teaspoons, or according to the desired size of the ravioli) on to a sheet of rolled-out pasta dough, about 2.5 cm (1 inch)

apart. Use a pastry brush to moisten the spaces between with water, then lay a second sheet of pasta dough over the first one. With your fingers, press the pasta between the mounds of filling and along the edges to stick the two sheets together, then cut between the piles of filling with a ravioli cutter, a fluted pastry cutter or simply a sharp knife.

Bring a large saucepan of salted water — about 2 litres (3½ pints) — to the boil. Add the pasta and cook at a gentle bubble until fairly soft to the bite — 10 to 15 minutes, depending on the size of the ravioli.

Meanwhile, prepare the sauce and the garnish. Dissolve the arrowroot in a little of the stock or water, combine it with the remaining stock or water and the two soaking liquids, and bring to the boil, stirring constantly. Reduce the heat and simmer until the sauce has thickened slightly, then beat in the remaining *fromage frais* and the tomato paste.

Cut the tomatoes into diamond shapes; tear the basil leaves roughly, leaving the smaller leaves whole. Drain the cooked ravioli thoroughly, and season with some black pepper. Place the ravioli in a warm serving bowl or in individual dishes, pour over the sauce, and garnish with the tomato pieces and basil.

Pork Balls with Angel's Hair Pasta

Serves 4
Working (and total) time: about 40 minutes

Calories **280**
Protein **20g**
Cholesterol **65mg**
Total fat **12g**
Saturated fat **6g**
Sodium **360mg**

250 g	pork fillet, trimmed of fat and minced	8 oz
1 tsp	fennel seeds	1 tsp
2 tbsp	finely chopped parsley	2 tbsp
1 tsp	fresh lemon juice	1 tsp
¼ tsp	salt	¼ tsp
	freshly ground black pepper	
1	bay leaf	1
1	onion	1
1	carrot	1
10	black peppercorns	10
30 cl	dry white wine	½ pint
2	fennel bulbs, feathery tops attached	2
150 g	capelli d'angelo (angel's hair pasta)	5 oz
30 g	unsalted butter	1 oz
1 tbsp	grated Parmesan cheese	1 tbsp

Combine the minced pork, fennel seeds, parsley and lemon juice, and season lightly with the salt and some pepper. Set the mixture aside.

To make a vegetable stock, put the bay leaf, onion, carrot, peppercorns and wine in a heavy-bottomed saucepan and cover with water. Bring to the boil, then reduce the heat to a simmer.

While the stock is simmering, wash the fennel and slice it very thinly, cutting out any stringy centre or tips; chop the feathery tops finely and reserve for garnishing the dish. With your hands, form the pork mixture into balls about the size of large marbles.

When the vegetable liquid has simmered for at least 10 minutes, plunge the fennel into the saucepan and simmer until it is cooked but still a little crunchy. Strain the contents of the pan; reserve the fennel and the liquid and discard the other ingredients. Return the liquid to the pan, simmer again and add the pork balls.

Bring a large saucepan of lightly salted water to the boil. Throw in the pasta and cook it until it is soft but still has a firm bite — about 4 minutes.

When the pork balls are cooked — about 5 minutes — add the fennel for a few seconds to warm through. Strain the pork and fennel, reserving about 4 tablespoons of the cooking liquid. Strain the pasta. Melt the butter in the larger saucepan, and add the pork, fennel and pasta. Divide the mixture among four warmed plates, pour a tablespoon of the reserved cooking liquid over each serving, and scatter the Parmesan and the reserved fennel fronds over the top. Serve immediately.

Saffron Pork with Quail and Prawns

Serves 4
Working (and total) time: about 1 hour

Calories **380**
Protein **22g**
Cholesterol **75mg**
Total fat **9g**
Saturated fat **3g**
Sodium **100mg**

250 g	pork fillet, trimmed of fat and cut into eight pieces	8 oz
2	quail	2
1 tbsp	virgin olive oil	1 tbsp
1	red onion, finely chopped	1
250 g	Italian round-grain rice	8 oz
¼ tsp	saffron powder	¼ tsp
2	pinches saffron threads	2
½ tsp	salt	½ tsp
	freshly ground black pepper	
1 to 1.25 litres	unsalted chicken stock (recipe, page 139) or water	1½ to 2 pints
1	green chili pepper, seeded and finely sliced (caution, page 36)	1
1	red chili pepper, seeded and finely sliced (caution, page 36)	1
4	large cooked prawns	4

Divide each quail in two by cutting down the back and up along the breastbone. Remove any innards that remain, wash the quail pieces and pat them dry with paper towels. Rub the quail with a little of the olive oil, then set aside.

Heat the remaining oil in a heavy paella pan or frying pan, and sweat the onion in it for 1 minute. Add the rice and sauté for about 1 minute, then add the pork and sauté the whole mixture for a further 2 minutes, until the pork is sealed. Add the saffron powder and saffron threads, season with the salt and some pepper, and pour on enough chicken stock or water to cover. Bring slowly to the boil, then simmer the mixture gently for 35 to 40 minutes, adding the remaining stock or water as necessary and stirring occasionally. After 30 minutes, test the rice for doneness. When it is still a little hard but nearly cooked, add the chili peppers and prawns to heat through.

While the rice mixture is cooking, grill the quail under a hot grill until they are well browned — about 10 minutes. Transfer the rice and pork mixture to a large dish or individual plates and serve immediately with the prawns and quail to one side.

Stuffed Pig's Trotters

Serves 8
Working time: about 1 hour and 30 minutes
Total time: about 10 hours (includes chilling)

Calories **220**
Protein **18g**
Cholesterol **100mg**
Total fat **16g**
Saturated fat **3g**
Sodium **160mg**

4	pig's trotters	4
2 tsp	salt	2 tsp
2	carrots, sliced	2
2	onions, peeled and stuck with three cloves each	2
2	sticks celery, sliced	2
1	bouquet garni	1
17.5 cl	dry white wine	6 fl oz
8 cl	wine vinegar	3 fl oz
Chicken and pistachio stuffing		
350 g	finely minced chicken breast	12 oz
1	garlic clove, crushed	1
2 tbsp	finely chopped parsley	2 tbsp
20 g	shelled pistachio nuts	¾ oz
2	egg yolks	2
	freshly ground black pepper	
Mustard vinaigrette		
1 tbsp	wine vinegar	1 tbsp
6 tbsp	safflower oil	6 tbsp
1 tsp	Dijon mustard	1 tsp
2 tbsp	finely chopped parsley	2 tbsp
1	garlic clove, crushed	1
½ tsp	salt	½ tsp
	freshly ground black pepper	
2 tbsp	finely chopped chives	2 tbsp
1 tbsp	chopped capers	1 tbsp
1 tbsp	finely chopped gherkin	1 tbsp

Singe the trotters over a naked flame, scrape off the burnt bristles and rub all over with the salt. Tie each trotter firmly between two strong wooden skewers *(Step 1, below)* and put them in a large pan with the carrots, onions, celery, bouquet garni, white wine and wine vinegar. Add water to cover and bring to the boil; cover tightly and simmer for 5½ hours.

Take the pan off the heat. Remove the trotters and set aside. Strain the stock, discard the solids and return the stock to the pan. Leave the trotters until they are cool enough to handle. Meanwhile, mix together all the stuffing ingredients until they are well blended.

Cut the strings round the trotters and take out all the bones *(Step 2)*. Sandwich the stuffing between the trotters as described in Step 3; wrap the muslin round the trotters and tie the ends to secure the package. Simmer the trotters for another hour in the stock.

Take the stuffed trotters out of the liquid to cool. Chill in the refrigerator for at least 2½ hours or preferably overnight. To prepare the vinaigrette, put the wine vinegar, oil, mustard, parsley, garlic, salt and some pepper in a jar and shake until they emulsify, then stir in the chives, capers and gherkin. When thoroughly chilled, unwrap the trotters and slice them thinly. Serve accompanied by the vinaigrette.

SUGGESTED ACCOMPANIMENT: *watercress and orange salad.*

Preparing Stuffed Trotters

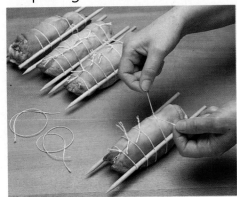

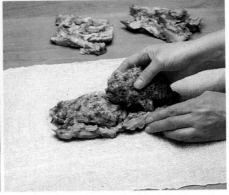

1 BRACING THE TROTTERS. To ensure that the trotters do not disintegrate while cooking, brace each one with two wooden skewers about 5 cm (2 inches) longer than the trotter. Secure the skewers with string tied round the trotters at intervals of about 2.5 cm (1 inch).

2 REMOVING THE BONES. After poaching the trotters in stock, cut away the string and discard the skewers. Split open each trotter lengthwise by cutting from the toes to the opposite end, then carefully pick out all the pieces of bone (above).

3 STUFFING THE TROTTERS. Lay two split trotters end to end on in the middle of a piece of muslin about 50 by 40 cm (20 by 16 inches). Spread a layer of prepared stuffing over the trotters, then place two more trotters split side down on top of the stuffing.

Roast Pork Salad with Mustard Vinaigrette

Serves 4
Working (and total) time: about 10 minutes

Calories **245**	350 g	cold roast pork	12 oz
Protein **26g**	125 g	salad lettuce leaves, washed and dried	4 oz
Cholesterol **60mg**	2 tsp	sherry vinegar	2 tsp
Total fat **14g**	2 tsp	fresh lemon juice	2 tsp
Saturated fat **4g**	2 tsp	Dijon mustard	2 tsp
Sodium **270mg**	1 tbsp	virgin olive oil	1 tbsp
	1 tbsp	arachide oil	1 tbsp
	15 g	chopped chives	1½ oz
	½ tsp	salt	½ tsp
		freshly ground black pepper	

Divide the lettuce leaves among four plates. Slice the pork as thinly as possible and lay it over the lettuce.

Whisk the sherry vinegar, lemon juice and mustard together in a bowl, then add the olive and arachide oils, and continue to whisk the mixture until it is thoroughly blended. Add the chopped chives and season with the salt and some freshly ground black pepper, then pour the mustard vinaigrette over the pork slices and lettuce.

SUGGESTED ACCOMPANIMENT: *crusty bread*.

Phyllo Parcels

Serves 4
Working time: about 45 minutes
Total time: about 4 hours (includes marinating)

Calories **280**
Protein **23g**
Cholesterol **70mg**
Total fat **15g**
Saturated fat **4g**
Sodium **100mg**

500 g	neck end or other lean pork, trimmed of fat and cut into 2 cm (¾ inch) cubes	1 lb
12.5 cl	red wine	4 fl oz
2	garlic cloves, crushed	2
1 tsp	fresh thyme leaves, bruised	1 tsp
1 tsp	mixed peppercorns, coarsely crushed	1 tsp
15 g	dried ceps	½ oz
½ tsp	salt	½ tsp
4	large spinach leaves, stalks removed, or about eight smaller leaves	4
2	sheets phyllo pastry, each about 50 by 28 cm (20 by 11 inches)	2
2 tbsp	safflower oil	2 tbsp
4 tsp	redcurrant jelly	4 tsp

Put the wine, garlic, thyme leaves and crushed peppercorns in a non-reactive dish and add the pork cubes. Cover the dish and leave to marinate in a cool place for at least 3 hours. Meanwhile, soak the ceps in warm water for 20 minutes.

Drain the meat and pat the cubes dry on paper towels. Reserve the little marinade that has not been absorbed. Drain the ceps, rinse them, then dry on paper towels and chop them roughly.

Sauté the meat in a dry non-stick frying pan over medium-high heat, turning regularly, for about 20 minutes, until the cubes are well browned on all sides and cooked through. Stir in the chopped mushrooms, the reserved marinade and the salt. Reduce the liquid so that the meat and mushrooms are completely dry, then remove the pan from the heat.

Plunge the spinach leaves into rapidly boiling water, drain immediately, refresh under cold running water and lay out in a single layer on several thicknesses of paper towels.

Preheat the oven to 190°C (375°F or Mark 5).

Cut each phyllo sheet lengthwise in half to make four long, broad strips. Position one strip with a short side towards you and brush it lightly with some of the oil. Place one large spinach leaf — or two or three smaller, overlapping leaves — at the end of the strip then a quarter of the meat mixture in a pile on the spinach. Lift one corner of the strip and fold it over the filling so that the corner meets the opposite long side, then fold the package towards the far end of the strip. Continue folding alternately across and up the strip until you reach the far end; any short band of phyllo remaining at the far end may be trimmed off or folded round the package. Repeat with the other strips and the rest of the spinach and meat.

Brush the packages lightly with the remaining oil and place them on a non-stick baking sheet. Bake in the oven for 20 minutes, turning once, until they are golden and crisp. Serve hot, with a spoonful of redcurrant jelly on the side.

SUGGESTED ACCOMPANIMENTS: *steamed broccoli; mashed potatoes.*

Cannelloni Stuffed with Pork and Ricotta

Serves 4
Working (and total) time: about 1 hour

Calories **460**
Protein **28g**
Cholesterol **45mg**
Total fat **20g**
Saturated fat **6g**
Sodium **145mg**

250 g	pork fillet, trimmed of fat and minced	8 oz
60 g	sun-dried tomatoes	2 oz
90 g	low-fat ricotta	3 oz
30 g	fresh basil, finely chopped	1 oz
	freshly ground black pepper	
8	cannelloni tubes	8
90 cl	unsalted vegetable or chicken stock (recipes, page 139)	1½ pints

Pesto sauce

90 g	fresh basil	3 oz
30 g	pine-nuts	1 oz
3 tbsp	virgin olive oil	3 tbsp
1	garlic clove	1
30 g	freshly grated Parmesan cheese	1 oz

Cut one of the sun-dried tomatoes into strips and reserve for a garnish. Chop the remaining tomatoes finely and mix them well with the pork, ricotta, basil and a little black pepper. Using your fingers, fill the cannelloni with this stuffing mixture.

To make the pesto, put the basil, pine-nuts, oil and garlic in a food processor or blender, and blend for 2 minutes. Add the Parmesan and blend again briefly.

Bring the stock to a simmer in a pan large enough to take the cannelloni in one layer. Using a slotted spoon, carefully put the cannelloni into the stock, and poach for 15 minutes, or until the pasta is soft and the stuffing feels firm. Drain, reserving the stock, and keep warm.

For the sauce, blend 4 tablespoons of the stock with 2 tablespoons of the pesto, and heat if necessary. Keep any remaining pesto for another use. Arrange the cannelloni on a warmed serving dish, pour a thick ribbon of pesto sauce over them and garnish with the reserved tomato strips.

EDITOR'S NOTE: *The cannelloni tubes used in this recipe do not require precooking before they are filled.*

Rocket Meatballs

Serves 4
Working time: about 25 minutes
Total time: about 40 minutes (includes marinating)

Calories **170**
Protein **22g**
Cholesterol **70mg**
Total fat **8g**
Saturated fat **3g**
Sodium **490mg**

500 g	shoulder or other lean pork for mincing, trimmed of fat	1 lb
30 g	rocket	1 oz
½ tsp	ground allspice	½ tsp
½ tsp	salt	½ tsp
	freshly ground black pepper	
4 tbsp	plain low-fat yogurt	4 tbsp
2 tsp	balsamic vinegar	2 tsp
Yogurt dip		
4 tbsp	plain low-fat yogurt	4 tbsp
2 tsp	balsamic vinegar	2 tsp
1 tsp	coriander seeds, toasted and crushed	1 tsp
¼ tsp	salt	¼ tsp

In a food processor, mince the pork with the rocket, allspice, salt and some pepper. Form into 16 small balls. Blend the yogurt and balsamic vinegar in a bowl and roll the balls in this mixture; leave them to marinate for 15 minutes, turning occasionally.

Preheat the grill to medium high. Place the meatballs and marinade in the grill pan and grill for about 10 minutes, turning and basting from time to time, until golden-brown and cooked through.

To make the dip, mix the cooking juices from the meatballs with the yogurt, balsamic vinegar, coriander and salt. Serve the meatballs hot with the yogurt dip in a bowl alongside.

SUGGESTED ACCOMPANIMENT: *green salad including rocket or watercress.*

EDITOR'S NOTE: *The meat used in this recipe should be very fresh, as this will require no binding agent. If rocket is unavailable, use watercress as a substitute — up to 60 g (2 oz) per 400 g (14 oz) of trimmed meat.*

Pork with Chinese Cabbage in Steamed Buns

Serves 6
Working time: about 50 minutes
Total time: about 2 hours and 20 minutes (includes proving)

Calories **340**
Protein **19g**
Cholesterol **30mg**
Total fat **14g**
Saturated fat **3g**
Sodium **450mg**

300 g	cooked roast pork loin, trimmed of fat and cut into small dice	10 oz
15 g	fresh yeast, or 7 g (¼ oz) dried yeast and ½ tsp sugar	½ oz
250 g	plain flour	8 oz
1 tsp	baking powder	1 tsp
15 g	hard white vegetable fat	½ oz
1 tbsp	sesame oil	1 tbsp
250 g	Chinese cabbage leaves, finely shredded	8 oz
1 tsp	salt	1 tsp
1 tbsp	safflower oil	1 tbsp
1 tsp	finely grated fresh ginger root	1 tsp
2	garlic cloves, finely chopped	2
90 g	spring onions, finely chopped	3 oz
1 tbsp	rice wine or dry sherry	1 tbsp
1 tbsp	low-sodium soy sauce or shoyu	1 tbsp
2 tbsp	hoisin or barbecue sauce	2 tbsp

Dissolve the yeast in 15 cl (¼ pint) of warm water; if using dried yeast, mix the sugar and yeast together with 15 cl (¼ pint) of warm water and leave for 10 minutes, until the mixture is foamy. Sift the flour and baking powder together into a large bowl, and rub in the fat. Mix the yeast liquid into the flour and fat and knead well. Cover the dough loosely with plastic film and leave until doubled in volume — about 1 hour.

Strike the dough with your hand to deflate it, then divide it into 12 balls. Roll out the balls into circles about 10 cm (4 inches) in diameter. Brush the dough circles lightly with a little of the sesame oil, then fold them over into semicircles and place each on a square of lightly oiled greaseproof paper. Cover loosely with plastic film and leave to rise again for 30 minutes. Steam the semicircles in a single layer, partially covered, over fiercely boiling water for 20 minutes.

Meanwhile, sprinkle the Chinese cabbage with the salt and set aside for 20 minutes. Rinse well under cold running water, then squeeze dry in your fist.

Heat the safflower oil in a small frying pan and fry the ginger, garlic and spring onions for 1 to 2 minutes, stirring all the time. Add the rice wine or sherry, soy sauce, hoisin or barbecue sauce and the remaining sesame oil, then reduce until the sauce is very thick and syrupy. Stir in the Chinese cabbage and the pork.

Serve the buns straight from the steamer with the hot pork mixture. Each diner takes a bun, splits it and spoons in some of the filling. Eat with the fingers.

EDITOR'S NOTE: *A bamboo steamer, as shown here, provides a wider, flatter surface for the buns than an ordinary steamer. It may be placed over a wok containing boiling water.*

Italian Meat Loaf with Tomato Sauce

Serves 6
Working time: about 25 minutes
Total time: about 1 hour and 10 minutes

Calories **250**
Protein **28g**
Cholesterol **80mg**
Total fat **11g**
Saturated fat **4g**
Sodium **130mg**

750 g	pork fillet, minced	1½ lb
1	garlic clove, chopped finely	1
30 g	fresh breadcrumbs	1 oz
1 tbsp	tomato paste	1 tbsp
2 tbsp	dry white wine	2 tbsp
30 g	sun-dried tomatoes, finely chopped	1 oz
30 g	fresh basil, finely chopped	1 oz
	freshly ground black pepper	

Tomato sauce

1 tbsp	virgin olive oil	1 tbsp
1	large onion, finely chopped	1
2	garlic cloves, finely chopped	2
1 kg	tomatoes, skinned and chopped, or 800 g (28 oz) canned plum tomatoes	2 lb
1	fresh bay leaf	1
2 tsp	finely chopped sun-dried tomatoes	2 tsp
	freshly ground black pepper	
45 g	dried ceps, soaked for 20 minutes in warm water, or 250 g (8 oz) fresh mushrooms, chopped and sautéed until soft in 15 g (½ oz) butter	1½ oz
30 g	fresh basil, torn into small pieces	1 oz

Preheat the oven to 180°C (350°F or Mark 4). Combine the pork, garlic and breadcrumbs with the tomato paste, wine, sun-dried tomatoes, basil and some pepper. Mix them well together. Line a 500 g (1 lb) loaf tin with greaseproof paper and press the pork mixture into it. Bake in the oven for 1 hour.

While the meat loaf is cooking, prepare the sauce. Heat the olive oil in a heavy frying pan and gently fry the onion and garlic until they are translucent — about 5 minutes. Add the tomatoes, bay leaf and the sun-dried tomatoes; season with some black pepper, and cook over medium heat for 15 to 20 minutes, or until the sauce is reduced and well combined. Drain the ceps, if using, and chop them into pieces of roughly equal size. When the sauce is cooked, remove the bay leaf from the pan and add the ceps or mushrooms and the basil. Reheat the sauce to warm through the ceps.

Serve the meat loaf cut into thick slices with the sauce spooned round it.

4 Tender pork chops cooked in the microwave oven with fennel are finished with an orange and Madeira glaze (recipe, opposite).

Pork in the Microwave Oven

Florence Fennel Chops

Serves 4

Working (and total) time: about 20 minutes

Calories **200**
Protein **25g**
Cholesterol **80mg**
Total fat **8g**
Saturated fat **3g**
Sodium **420mg**

4	boned loin chops (about 125 g/ 4 oz each), trimmed of fat	4
2	fennel bulbs (about 150 g/5 oz each)	2
3 tbsp	fresh orange juice	3 tbsp
1 tbsp	Madeira	1 tbsp
½ tsp	arrowroot	½ tsp
15 cl	unsalted vegetable stock (recipe, page 139)	¼ pint
1 tsp	salt	1 tsp
	freshly ground white pepper	
½ tsp	ground fennel seed (optional)	½ tsp
	Orange glaze	
1 tbsp	fresh orange juice	1 tbsp
1 tsp	finely grated orange rind	1 tsp
1 tbsp	clear honey	1 tbsp
1 tbsp	Madeira	1 tbsp
1 tbsp	balsamic vinegar	1 tbsp

The advantages of the microwave oven in terms of convenience for the cook are well known — it cooks food far more rapidly than a conventional oven or hob, it is easy to clean and cheap to run, and it takes up very little space in the kitchen. The recipes in this chapter have been chosen to demonstrate that there are benefits for the diner also, and that the appearance and flavour of certain dishes are actually improved by cooking in the microwave oven.

Because the process of mincing breaks down the meat's fibres, minced pork is particularly suited to rapid cooking in the microwave oven. Chops also benefit from microwave cooking. When chops are fried or grilled, the time required for the meat round the bone to cook through properly can cause the outside to become dried out and tough; in the microwave the chops will cook through evenly, so that the inside will be ready at the same time as the outside.

The speed of microwave cooking is most evident in the case of stews and casserole dishes. The recipe for pork in cider on page 131, for example, requires only 15 minutes in the microwave oven plus 5 minutes for thickening the liquid, and all other casserole recipes in this chapter can be cooked in under an hour. A microwave oven also provides the quickest means of preparing the constituent ingredients — such as the winter squash in the golden casserole on page 133 — and of reheating a casserole cooked in advance.

Several of the recipes call for the use of a browning dish, a glass-ceramic grill or dish with a tin-oxide coating that colours the meat in the same way as the initial searing at high temperatures in conventional cooking. Always follow the manufacturer's instructions strictly when using this dish, as overheating can damage it. Also, when covering a microwave dish containing liquid with greaseproof paper or microwave-safe plastic film, take care to leave one corner loose to prevent a build-up of steam.

The recipes have been tested in 650-watt and 700-watt ovens. Power settings often vary among different microwave ovens, but in the recipes that follow "high" indicates 100 per cent power, "medium high" 70 per cent, "medium" 50 per cent and "medium low" 30 per cent power. Because food continues to cook for a short while after it is removed from the oven, it is important to guard against overcooking by using the shortest time specified. You can then test for doneness after resting the dish for a minute or so, and return it to the oven if necessary.

Divide each fennel bulb into eight sections. Place them in a dish with the orange juice and Madeira and microwave on high until barely tender — 7 to 8 minutes.

Preheat a browning dish on high for 5 to 7 minutes, or the maximum time allowed by the manufacturer. Dry the chops and arrange them in the browning dish, thickest part to the outside, pressing them down hard on to the browning surface with a spatula. Once the sizzling stops, cook the chops on high for 1 minute then turn them over to lightly brown the other side.

Mix the arrowroot with the stock and stir into the fennel. Pour the mixture round the chops and cook on high until the liquid begins to bubble and thicken slightly — about 1 minute. Stir well, reduce to medium and cook, covered, until tender — 2 to 3 minutes. Stir gently and give the dish a quarter turn every minute.

Remove the dish from the oven and leave to rest for 2 minutes. Test for doneness by cutting through the thickest part of a chop with the point of a sharp knife; if the meat appears pink, cook for just 1 minute more on medium, and test as before. Repeat as necessary, taking care not to overcook. When fully cooked, rest the chops for 2 to 3 minutes while making the glaze.

Combine the glaze ingredients in a dish of a volume at least double that of the liquid. Cook on high until the glaze is of a syrupy, coating consistency — 2½ to 3 minutes. Brush some glaze over the chops. Add the remaining glaze to the fennel sauce and cook on high for ½ to 1 minute, stirring half way through. Season with the salt, some pepper, and the fennel seed, if using. Serve the chops with their sauce immediately.

Stuffed Chops with Kidney Bean and Juniper Sauce

Serves 4
Working time: about 20 minutes
Total time: about 35 minutes

Calories **425**
Protein **40g**
Cholesterol **70mg**
Total fat **15g**
Saturated fat **5g**
Sodium **110mg**

4	pork chops (about 125 to 150 g/ 4½ to 5 oz each), trimmed of fat	4
30 g	pine-nuts	1 oz
60 g	cooked long-grain rice	2 oz
4	fresh dates, stoned	4
½ tsp	dried rosemary	½ tsp
1 tsp	safflower oil	1 tsp
Kidney bean and juniper sauce		
250 g	cooked kidney beans	8 oz
¼ tsp	freshly ground black pepper	¼ tsp
18	juniper berries	18
30 cl	unsalted vegetable stock (recipe, page 139)	½ pint
2 tbsp	tomato paste	2 tbsp

In a food processor, blend together the pine-nuts, rice, dates and rosemary. (Alternatively, chop the rice, dates and pine-nuts, and mix them by hand with the rosemary.) Cut a cavity in the side of each of the chops, and press the stuffing mixture into the cavities, as demonstrated on page 12, below.

Preheat a browning dish for 5 to 7 minutes, or for the maximum time allowed in the manufacturer's instructions, and swirl the oil round the base of the dish. Pat the chops dry with paper towels to facilitate browning, and arrange them in the dish with the thickest part to the outside, pressing them down on to the browning surface with a spatula. When the sizzling stops, cook the chops on high for 1 minute before turning them over to brown the other side.

To make the sauce, purée the kidney beans, pepper, juniper berries, stock and tomato paste in a food processor or blender. Pour into a shallow dish and arrange the chops over the purée with the thicker part towards the outside of the dish.

Microwave on high, uncovered, until the chops are just cooked — about 7 minutes. Remove the chops from the dish and keep them warm.

Return the dish to the microwave and cook the sauce on high for 3 minutes to reduce and thicken it, stirring once during cooking. Pour the sauce on to the chops and serve immediately.

SUGGESTED ACCOMPANIMENTS: *broccoli florets; creamed potatoes and microwaved tomato halves.*

Celery Chops

Serves 4
Working time: about 15 minutes
Total time: about 40 minutes

Calories **200**
Protein **25g**
Cholesterol **70mg**
Total fat **9g**
Saturated fat **4g**
Sodium **390mg**

4	boneless loin chops (about 125 g/4 oz each), trimmed of fat	4
350 g	celery, cut into 2.5 cm (1 inch) pieces	12 oz
15 cl	stout	¼ pint
15 cl	unsalted vegetable stock (recipe, page 139)	¼ pint
½	onion, sliced	½
1 tsp	arrowroot, dissolved in 1 tbsp stout, stock or water	1 tsp
90 g	smetana	3 oz
1 to 2 tbsp	prepared English grainy mustard	1 to 2 tbsp
1 tbsp	torn lovage leaves	1 tbsp
1 tbsp	torn celery leaves	1 tbsp
½ tsp	salt	½ tsp
	freshly ground black pepper	

Place the celery in a dish with the stout, stock and onion. Bring to the boil on high, then cook on high for 10 to 15 minutes, or until tender.

Preheat a browning dish on high for 5 to 7 minutes, or for the maximum time allowed in the manufacturer's instructions. Quickly arrange the chops in the dish with the thickest part to the outside and press down hard on to the browning surface with a spatula. Once the sizzling stops, cook the chops on high for 1 minute, then turn them over to brown the other side lightly.

Pour the celery and cooking liquid round the chops and cook on high for another minute, or until the liquid bubbles. Reduce the setting to medium and cook for 3 minutes, covered, giving the dish a quarter turn every minute. Allow to rest for 2 minutes, then test for doneness by cutting through the thickest part of a chop with the point of a sharp knife; if the meat is still pink, cook for 1 minute more and test as before. Repeat as necessary, but take care not to overcook. When fully cooked, drain the pork and celery, reserving the cooking liquid, and keep warm while you make the sauce.

Beat the arrowroot mixture into the smetana, then add 1 tablespoon each of the mustard and reserved cooking liquid, stirring well. Cook on high for 1 to 2 minutes, until thickened, stirring every 20 seconds or so. Add the lovage and celery, the salt, some pepper, and the remaining mustard to taste. Pour the sauce over the pork and celery and serve immediately.

SUGGESTED ACCOMPANIMENTS: *baked potatoes; glazed carrots.*

Winter Fruited Chops

Serves 4
Working (and total) time: about 30 minutes

Calories **180**
Protein **25g**
Cholesterol **70mg**
Total fat **8g**
Saturated fat **3g**
Sodium **260mg**

4	loin chops (about 125 to 150g/ 4½ to 5 oz each), trimmed of fat	4
2 tbsp	prepared English grainy mustard	2 tbsp
12	fresh sage leaves	12
½ tsp	salt	½ tsp
2	slices Seville orange, halved	2
2 tsp	fine mustard powder (optional)	2 tsp
4 tbsp	cranberry sauce or preserve	4 tbsp
200 g	fresh cranberries, chopped	7 oz
2 tbsp	port	2 tbsp
	freshly ground black pepper	

Cut a pocket in the boneless side of each chop *(page 12)*. Spread ½ tablespoon of the mustard over the surfaces of each pocket, and press three sage leaves on to the mustard. Sprinkle with a little of the salt, and place a half slice of orange in each pocket.

Dust one side of each chop with ½ teaspoon of the mustard powder, if you are using it. Spread 1 tablespoon of the cranberry sauce over the powdered side of each chop and press the fresh berries firmly into the preserve.

Arrange the chops in a dish with the thickest part towards the outside of the dish. Microwave on medium for 4 minutes, turning the dish once during this time, then rearrange the chops with a spatula to ensure that they will be evenly cooked. Cook for a further 6 to 8 minutes on medium, giving the dish a quarter turn at least three times during this period.

Remove the chops from the oven, rest them in their dish for 2 minutes, then test for doneness by cutting into the bone end of a chop with the point of a sharp knife; if no pink meat is visible (allowing for pink staining by the fruit juice), the chops are cooked through. If the meat still appears pink, cook for a further 1 to 2 minutes on medium, then test as before. Remove the chops from the dish and keep them warm.

To make a quick, light sauce, reduce the cooking juices in the dish by microwaving on high for 2 to 3 minutes; add the port wine and reduce further on high until slightly syrupy in appearance. Season with the remaining salt and some freshly ground black pepper, and spoon over the chops.

EDITOR'S NOTE: *If a slightly sweeter flavour is preferred to balance the sourness of the cranberries, spread a little orange jelly or light brown sugar over the orange slices and cranberries. To make a summer variant of this dish, use 2 tablespoons of redcurrant jelly, 100 g (3½ oz) of fresh redcurrants, sweet orange slices and fresh lovage leaves in place of the fresh cranberries and sage.*

Chops with Aubergine Purée and Vegetables

Serves 4
Working (and total) time: about 45 minutes

Calories **250**
Protein **26g**
Cholesterol **70mg**
Total fat **13g**
Saturated fat **3g**
Sodium **370mg**

4	boned loin chops (about 125 g/ 4 oz each), trimmed of fat	4
500 g	aubergines	1 lb
1 tsp	safflower oil	1 tsp
90 g	thick Greek yogurt	3 oz
1 tsp	salt	1 tsp
½ tsp	ground coriander	½ tsp
¼ tsp	ground cumin	¼ tsp
4	small fresh mint sprigs	4
	freshly ground black pepper	
	Mediterranean vegetables	
2	courgettes, sliced	2
1	sweet red pepper, seeded, deribbed and sliced	1
1	sweet yellow pepper, seeded, deribbed and sliced	1
1	tomato, sliced	1
1 tbsp	safflower oil	1 tbsp
½	garlic clove, finely chopped	½
1 tbsp	finely chopped coriander	1 tbsp

Pierce the skin of the aubergines in several places with the point of a sharp knife. Brush the skin with about ½ teaspoon of the oil, place the aubergines on a double thickness of absorbent paper towels and cook on high for 5 minutes, turning twice during this time.

The aubergines should be soft, but not collapsed, and the skin fairly tender. When they are cool enough to handle, slice them into 2 cm (¾ inch) thick rounds.

Preheat a browning dish on high for 5 to 7 minutes, or for the maximum time allowed in the manufacturer's instructions. Pat the chops dry with paper towels to facilitate browning and brush them with the remaining oil. When the browning dish is ready, quickly arrange the chops in it with the thickest part to the outside of the dish; press down hard with a spatula. Once the sizzling stops, cook the chops on high for 1 minute, then turn them over to lightly brown the other side.

Remove the chops and arrange the aubergine slices in the dish. Place the chops on top of the aubergines. Cover the dish with a lid or with greaseproof paper, and cook on medium for 5 minutes, giving the dish a quarter turn every minute. Allow to rest for 2 minutes, then test for doneness by cutting through the thickest part of a chop with the point of a sharp knife; if the meat is still pink, cook for 1 minute more on medium and test as before. Repeat the process as necessary, but take care not to overcook the chops. When fully cooked, remove the chops and keep them warm.

To prepare the vegetables, mix together the courgettes, sweet peppers and tomato with the safflower oil, garlic and chopped coriander. Microwave on high for 3 minutes.

To prepare the purée, blend or process together the aubergine, yogurt, salt, ground coriander, cumin and mint. The purée should still be quite thick; if you wish, add any cooking juices which the aubergine did not absorb. Season with some black pepper and serve warm with the chops and vegetables.

Pork and Barley Hotpot

Serves 8
Working time: about 35 minutes
Total time: about 9 hours (includes soaking)

Calories **165**
Protein **13g**
cholesterol **45mg**
Total fat **6g**
Saturated fat **2g**
Sodium **75mg**

500 g	pork fillet, trimmed of fat and cut into 2.5 cm (1 inch) cubes	1 lb
90 g	pot barley	3 oz
60 cl	unsalted chicken stock (recipe, page 139)	1 pint
1 tbsp	safflower oil	1 tbsp
250 g	pearl onions, peeled	8 oz
1 tbsp	dark brown sugar	1 tbsp
250 g	carrots, cut into bâtonnets	8 oz
7	dried lemon verbena leaves	7
	freshly ground black pepper	
125 g	French beans, topped and tailed	4 oz
1 tbsp	cornflour	1 tbsp
125 g	shelled peas, or frozen peas, thawed	4 oz

Put the barley and stock in a covered bowl and refrigerate overnight to soften and swell the barley.

The next day, put the oil in a large casserole dish with the onions and sugar, stir well and microwave on high until the onions brown slightly — about 5 minutes. Add the pork and microwave on high for 3 minutes, stirring once, to lightly seal the meat. Stir in the undrained barley, carrots, lemon verbena and some pepper. Cover the dish and microwave on high for about 15 minutes, until the meat and vegetables are almost tender; stir occasionally. Add the beans about 4 minutes before the end of the cooking time.

Blend the cornflour with 2 tablespoons of water and stir into the hotpot. Without covering, microwave on high until the liquid boils — about 3 minutes. Remove from the oven, add the peas and stir well; leave for 1 to 2 minutes to cook the peas, then serve.

Cider Pork

Serves 6
Working time: about 25 minutes
Total time: about 4 hours and 30 minutes (includes marinating)

Calories **195**
Protein **17g**
Cholesterol **70mg**
Total fat **10g**
Saturated fat **4g**
Sodium **80mg**

750 g	pork fillet, trimmed of fat and cut into 2.5 cm (1 inch) cubes	1½ lb
1	garlic clove, crushed	1
1 tbsp	walnut oil	1 tbsp
15 cl	medium dry cider	¼ pint
1	orange, grated rind and juice	1
2 tsp	fresh lemon juice	2 tsp
1 tbsp	fresh thyme, or 1 tsp dried thyme	1 tbsp
½ tsp	grated fresh ginger root	½ tsp
½ tsp	freshly ground black pepper	½ tsp
4 tsp	arrowroot, dissolved in 3 tbsp cider	4 tsp

In a large casserole, mix together all the ingredients except the pork and the arrowroot mixture. Stir in the pork, cover and leave to marinate in the refrigerator for 4 to 6 hours. Stir the meat once or twice during this time to make sure the cubes are evenly soaked.

Put the covered casserole in the oven and microwave on medium until the meat is tender — about 10 minutes. Stir once during cooking. Pour the arrowroot and cider mixture into the casserole and microwave on high, stirring once during cooking, until the liquid thickens — about 5 minutes. Serve hot.

SUGGESTED ACCOMPANIMENT: *saffron rice.*

Greek Casserole

Serves 4
Working time: about 15 minutes
Total time: about 1 hour

Calories **290**
Protein **23g**
Cholesterol **70mg**
Total fat **8g**
Saturated fat **3g**
Sodium **400 mg**

400 g	lean roasting pork, cut into 2.5 cm (1 inch) cubes	14 oz
1 tbsp	potato flour, seasoned with white pepper	1 tbsp
1 tsp	virgin olive oil	1 tsp
30 cl	unsalted veal or vegetable stock (recipes, page 139)	½ pint
350 g	small (2.5 cm/1 inch) new potatoes, or larger potatoes cut into 2.5 cm (1 inch) cubes	12 oz
4	dried pear halves	4
2 tbsp	chunky quince preserve	2 tbsp
2 tbsp	honey, preferably Hymettus	2 tbsp
4	fresh thyme sprigs	4
½	cinnamon stick	½
2	5 cm (2 inch) strips lemon rind	2
20 cl	retsina	7 fl oz
1 tsp	salt	1 tsp
4 to 6 tbsp	fresh lemon juice	4 to 6 tbsp
	freshly ground black pepper	

Preheat a browning dish on high for 5 to 7 minutes, or for the maximum time allowed in the manufacturer's instructions. Toss the cubes of meat in the seasoned flour. Brush the browning dish with the oil and add the meat. Cook on high for 2 minutes, stirring frequently so that the meat browns evenly.

Heat the stock until it is almost boiling. Add 8 cl (3 fl oz) of the stock to the meat and cook for 2 minutes more on high, scraping the dish with a spatula to detach the brown sediment and thicken the sauce. Add the potatoes, pears, quince preserve, honey, thyme, cinnamon, lemon rind and retsina, and enough stock to cover the meat (which may otherwise discolour slightly). Continue to cook on high until the liquid comes to the boil — 10 to 15 minutes. Stir the contents of the dish; cover and cook for another 30 to 45 minutes on medium low, until the meat is tender. Stir the contents of the dish once or twice during this time and add more stock if the liquid in the dish falls below the level of the meat.

Towards the end of the cooking time, add the salt and sufficient lemon juice to cut the sweetness pleasantly; a little more honey may be added if a sweeter taste is desired. Remove the cinnamon and thyme, season with some pepper and serve hot.

Golden Casserole

THIS NOURISHING DISH MAKES A COMPLETE MEAL AND NEEDS
NO ACCOMPANIMENT.

Serves 4
Working time: about 30 minutes
Total time: about 1 hour and 30 minutes

Calories **270**
Protein **24g**
Cholesterol **70mg**
Total fat **8g**
Saturated fat **3g**
Sodium **300mg**

400 g	pork fillet, trimmed of fat and cut into 2.5 cm (1 inch) cubes	14 oz
1 tbsp	safflower oil	1 tbsp
300 g	acorn, butternut or other winter squash	10 oz
400 g	sweet potatoes or eddoes, or a mixture of the two	14 oz
¼ tsp	saffron threads	¼ tsp
½ tsp	crystal salt	½ tsp
30 cl	unsalted vegetable stock (recipe, page 139)	½ pint
1	blade mace	1
2	whole allspice berries	2
300 g	custard marrows, yellow courgettes or other summer squash	10 oz
100 g	baby sweetcorn	3½ oz
¼ tsp	salt	¼ tsp

Preheat a browning dish for 5 to 7 minutes, or for the maximum time allowed in the manufacturer's instructions. Add the oil and the pork and stir vigorously for about 1½ minutes until the meat is lightly browned. Transfer the meat to a casserole dish.

Pierce the skin of the acorn or butternut squash in two or three places with a skewer or sharp knife, then microwave it on high, on a double thickness of paper towels, for 5 minutes — it will now be softened and easy to cut. Peel and cut into 2.5 cm (1 inch) cubes.

Peel the sweet potatoes or eddoes, dice them into 2.5 cm (1 inch) cubes, and place them in the casserole dish with the meat. Using a mortar and pestle, grind the saffron with the crystal salt until pulverized. Warm the stock, dissolve the saffron and salt in it and pour the liquid into the casserole. Add the mace and allspice and microwave on high until the liquid begins to boil — about 5 minutes. Stir and cook for a further 15 minutes on medium low.

Remove the casserole from the microwave and add the acorn or butternut squash. Cook for a further 10 minutes on medium low.

Cut the custard marrows or courgettes into pieces slightly smaller than the rest of the vegetables and the meat. Wash the baby sweetcorn, keeping these whole if under 5 cm (2 inches) in length. Add the custard marrows or courgettes and sweetcorn to the casserole and cook for a final 10 minutes on medium low.

Remove the mace and allspice and add the salt. The golden liquid will be clear and thin. Serve hot.

EDITOR'S NOTE: *In place of the fillet, you can substitute a more dense, muscular cut such as neck end or the fillet end of leg in this recipe. Trim the meat of all visible fat, and allow about 15 minutes longer cooking time before adding the custard marrow or courgettes and sweetcorn.*

Kofta with Curry Sauce and Cucumber

COMMON IN INDIAN AND MIDDLE EASTERN COOKERY, KOFTA
CONSISTS OF MINCED MEAT WITH SEASONINGS SHAPED INTO
BALLS OR SAUSAGE SHAPES.

Serves 8
Working (and total) time: about 55 minutes

Calories **230**
Protein **22g**
Cholesterol **65mg**
Total fat **11g**
Saturated fat **3g**
Sodium **275mg**

750 g	trimmed leg or neck end of pork, minced	1 ½ lb
¼ tsp	chili powder	¼ tsp
1 ½ tsp	ground turmeric	1 ½ tsp
1 tsp	ground cardamom	1 tsp
½ tsp	salt	½ tsp
1 cm	piece fresh ginger root, chopped	½ inch
2 tbsp	besan flour or soya flour	2 tbsp
2 tsp	finely chopped coriander leaves	2 tsp
1 tsp	finely chopped parsley sprigs	1 tsp
250 g	cucumber, sliced into 4 cm (1 ½ inch) lengths and quartered	8 oz
Curry sauce		
2 tbsp	safflower oil	2 tbsp
250 g	onions, very finely chopped	8 oz
1	garlic clove, crushed	1
2.5 cm	piece cinnamon stick	1 inch
4	cloves	4
2 tbsp	ground coriander	2 tbsp
2 tbsp	ground cumin	2 tbsp
¼ tsp	chili powder	¼ tsp
1	bay leaf	1
½ tsp	salt	½ tsp
250 g	potatoes, grated	8 oz
500 g	ripe tomatoes, skinned and seeded, or 250 g canned whole tomatoes	1 lb

To prepare the sauce, first preheat a large browning dish for 5 to 7 minutes, or for the maximum time allowed in the manufacturer's instructions. Add the oil and onion and microwave, uncovered, on high, stirring occasionally, until the onions are softened and slightly brown — about 5 minutes. Stir in the garlic, cinnamon stick, cloves, coriander, cumin, chili powder, bay leaf and salt, and microwave on high for 30 seconds. Add the potatoes, tomatoes and 45 cl (¾ pint) of water; cover and cook on high for 20 minutes, stirring occasionally; if covering with plastic film, leave a corner open to allow steam to escape.

While the sauce is cooking, put the chili powder, turmeric, cardamom, salt, ginger and flour into a bowl, add the chopped coriander and parsley, and mix together. Shape the mixture into 16 sausage shapes or balls and set them aside.

When the sauce ingredients have cooked, purée them in a food processor or blender, pass them through a sieve, then return the sauce to the dish. Arrange the kofta in the dish, cover and microwave on high for 5 minutes. Rearrange the kofta, exchanging those in the centre with the ones round the edges. Baste the kofta with the sauce and microwave on high for 2 minutes, then add the cucumber pieces and cook for 1 minute more.

SUGGESTED ACCOMPANIMENTS: *poppadoms; boiled rice.*

EDITOR'S NOTE: *Besan flour is made from ground chick-peas and lentils. Poppadoms may be cooked in the microwave oven on high until they are puffy — about 1 minute.*

Herbed Scrolls with Leek

Serves 4
Working (and total) time: about 40 minutes

Calories **250**
Protein **21g**
Cholesterol **70mg**
Total fat **12g**
Saturated fat **3g**
Sodium **110mg**

400 g	pork fillet, trimmed of fat	14 oz
1	large leek	1
1	egg white	1
½ tsp	salt	½ tsp
60 g	fromage frais	2 oz
60 g	low-fat ricotta cheese	2 oz
3 tbsp	finely chopped mixed fresh herbs	3 tbsp
1 tbsp	herbed oil or virgin olive oil	1 tbsp
Honey glaze		
4 tbsp	clear honey	4 tbsp
1 tbsp	fresh lime or lemon juice	1 tbsp
1 tbsp	fresh orange juice	1 tbsp
1 tbsp	balsamic vinegar	1 tbsp
1 tbsp	low-sodium soy sauce or shoyu	1 tbsp
2	fresh thyme sprigs	2
1 tsp	arrowroot, dissolved in a little orange juice or water	1 tsp

Cut the fillet on the slant into 20 thin rounds, then beat out the rounds with a wooden mallet, until three times their original size *(page 12, above)*. Set aside.

Cut off two or three of the outer leaves of the leek and wash them carefully. Blanch the leaves for 2 minutes on high in lightly salted, boiling water, then rinse in cold water and spread them out on paper towels to dry. Finely slice the white part of the leek, blanch for 2 to 3 minutes, and drain thoroughly.

Whisk the egg white with the salt until fairly stiff. In another bowl, beat together the cheeses, mixed herbs and the white slices of leek, then fold in the egg white. Divide this mixture among the pieces of fillet, leaving a narrow border round the edges. Roll up the fillet pieces and leave them on a plate, seam side down. Cut the leek leaves into 20 strips about 1 cm (½ inch) wide and tie the stuffed scrolls with these ribbons, with the knot on top and the seam underneath.

Preheat a browning dish on high for 5 to 7 minutes, or for the maximum time allowed in the manufacturer's instructions. Swirl the oil round the base of the dish, and carefully arrange the scrolls in the dish, seam side down and radiating outwards like spokes of a wheel. Microwave on high for 1 minute; turn the scrolls over, using tongs, and cook for a further 2 minutes on high, turning both the scrolls and the dish at least twice during this time. Allow to rest for 30 seconds, then remove one of the scrolls and cut it in half to check for doneness. If no pink meat is visible, the scrolls are cooked; otherwise cook for a further 30 seconds on high, rest the scrolls for a few seconds, and test again.

To make the glaze, combine all the ingredients except the arrowroot mixture and cook on high for 3 minutes. Remove the thyme sprigs. If the glaze is not yet of a coating consistency, stir the arrowroot mixture into the glaze and cook on high for a further 45 sec-

onds, stirring half way through. Brush the scrolls with the glaze, and serve at once.

SUGGESTED ACCOMPANIMENTS: *lightly cooked carrots or baby leeks; tiny new potatoes.*

EDITOR'S NOTE: *For the mixed fresh herbs, use a selection of the following: tarragon, basil, chervil, marjoram, oregano, thyme, mint, sage, lovage and sorrel. If you wish, you can omit the glaze and season the scrolls simply with a little salt and freshly ground pepper.*

Stewed Fennel with Ham

Serves 4
Working time: about 5 minutes
Total time: about 20 minutes

Calories **130**
Protein **8g**
Cholesterol **30mg**
Total fat **10g**
Saturated fat **4g**
Sodium **315mg**

125 g	ham, trimmed of fat	4 oz
8	fennel bulbs	8
1 tbsp	finely chopped fresh thyme, or 1 tsp dried thyme	1 tbsp
12.5 cl	white wine	4 fl oz
4 tbsp	unsalted vegetable stock (recipe, page 139)	4 tbsp
	freshly ground black pepper	
30 g	unsalted butter (optional)	1 oz

Cut a thin slice off the root of each fennel bulb and trim off the tops of the stems; reserve the feathery fronds.

Put the fennel bulbs, thyme, white wine, vegetable stock, some freshly ground black pepper and the butter, if you are using it, into a dish. Cover and microwave on high until the fennel is cooked through — about 15 minutes.

Meanwhile, cut the ham into fine dice, and add it to the dish 1 minute before the end of the cooking time. Serve garnished with the feathery tops of the fennel, torn into small pieces.

SUGGESTED ACCOMPANIMENTS: *plain boiled rice; green salad.*

EDITOR'S NOTE: *Chicory or onions can be substituted for the fennel bulbs with equally good results. Allow two whole vegetables per person and cook for only 10 minutes; garnish with chopped parsley.*

Vine Leaves Stuffed with Pork and Rice

Serves 4
Working (and total) time: about 30 minutes

Calories **220**
Protein **15g**
Cholesterol **45mg**
Total fat **12g**
Saturated fat **4g**
Sodium **250 mg**

250 g	trimmed leg or neck end of pork, minced	8 oz
12	large fresh vine leaves	12
90 g	cooked brown rice	3 oz
2 tsp	dried oregano	2 tsp
¼ tsp	salt	¼ tsp
	freshly ground black pepper	
1 tbsp	fresh lemon juice	1 tbsp
2 tbsp	virgin olive oil	2 tbsp
30 cl	unsalted chicken stock (recipe, page 139)	½ pint
	lemon slices for garnish	

Put the vine leaves in a bowl and cover generously with water. Microwave on high until boiling — about 5 minutes. Leave the bowl to stand for 10 minutes, then remove the vine leaves and trim away the stalks.

Mix together the minced pork, brown rice, oregano, salt and some freshly ground pepper. Place a spoonful of the pork mixture in the centre of each leaf, wrap one end of the leaf over the filling, then the two sides, and roll up into a neat parcel.

Pack the rolled vine leaves tightly in a single layer in an oval casserole dish, with their seams underneath. Pour over the lemon juice, oil and stock, which should almost cover the parcels. Cover the dish and microwave on medium for 10 minutes.

Serve the stuffed vine leaves hot or cold, garnished with the lemon slices. If serving hot, the cooking liquid may be poured over them.

SUGGESTED ACCOMPANIMENTS: *lettuce and tomato salad sprinkled with feta cheese; crusty bread.*

EDITOR'S NOTE: *If you use vine leaves preserved in brine instead of fresh leaves, rinse them first under running cold water to remove the salt.*

Chicken Stock

Makes 2 to 3 litres (3½ to 5 pints)
Working time: about 20 minutes
Total time: about 3 hours

2 to 2.5 kg	uncooked chicken trimmings and bones (preferably wings, necks and backs), the bones cracked with a heavy knife	4 to 5 lb
2	carrots, scrubbed, sliced into 1 cm (½ inch) rounds)	2
3	sticks celery, sliced into 2.5 cm (1 inch) lengths	3
2	large onions, cut in half, one half stuck with 2 cloves	2
2	fresh thyme sprigs, or ½ tsp dried thyme	2
1 or 2	bay leaves	1 or 2
10 to 15	parsley stems	10 to 15
5	black peppercorns	5

Put the trimmings and bones in a heavy stock-pot and pour in enough water to cover them by 5 cm (2 inches). Slowly bring the liquid to the boil, skimming off the scum that rises to the surface. Boil for 10 minutes, skimming and adding a little cold water from time to time to help precipitate the scum.

Add the vegetables, herbs and peppercorns, and submerge them in the liquid. If necessary, add enough additional water to cover the vegetables and bones. Reduce the heat to low. Simmer the mixture for 2 to 3 hours, skimming once more during the process.

Strain the stock and allow it to stand until tepid, then refrigerate it overnight or freeze it long enough for the fat to congeal. Spoon off and discard the layer of fat.

Tightly covered and refrigerated, the stock may safely be kept for three to four days. Stored in small, tightly covered freezer containers and frozen, the stock may be kept for as long as six months.

EDITOR'S NOTE: *The chicken gizzard and heart may be added to the stock. Wings and necks — rich in gelatine — produce a particularly gelatinous stock, ideal for sauces and jellied dishes. The liver should never be used.*

Veal Stock

Makes about 3 litres (5 pints)
Working time: about 30 minutes
Total time: about 4 hours and 30 minutes

1.5 kg	veal breast or shin meat, cut into 7.5 cm (3 inch) pieces	3 lb
1.5 kg	veal bones (preferably knuckles), cracked	3 lb
2	onions, quartered	2
2	sticks celery, sliced	2
1	carrot, sliced	1
8	black peppercorns	8
3	unpeeled garlic cloves (optional), crushed	3
1 tsp	fresh thyme, or ¼ tsp dried thyme	1 tsp
1	bay leaf	1

Fill a large pot half way with water. Bring the water to the boil, add the veal meat and bones, and blanch them for 2 minutes to clean them. Drain the meat and bones in a colander, discarding the liquid. Rinse the meat and bones under cold running water and return them to the pot.

Add the onions, celery, carrot, peppercorns, and garlic if you are using it. Pour in enough water to cover the contents of the pot by about 7.5 cm (3 inches), and bring the water to the boil over medium heat. Reduce the heat to maintain a simmer, and skim any impurities from the surface. Add the thyme and bay leaf, and simmer very gently for 4 hours, skimming occasionally.

Strain the stock into a large bowl, then cool it as for chicken stock and spoon off the congealed fat.

Tightly covered and refrigerated, the stock may safely be kept for three to four days. Stored in small, tightly covered freezer containers and frozen, the stock may be kept for as long as six months.

EDITOR'S NOTE: *Any combination of veal meat and bones may be used to make this stock; ideally, the meat and bones together should weigh about 3 kg (6 lb). Ask your butcher to crack the bones.*

Vegetable Stock

Makes about 1½ litres (2½ pints)
Working time: about 25 minutes
Total time: about 1 hour and 30 minutes

3	sticks celery with leaves, finely chopped	3
3	carrots, scrubbed, sliced into 3 mm (⅛ inch) rounds	3
3	large onions (about 750 g/ 1½ lb), coarsely chopped	3
2	large broccoli stems, coarsely chopped (optional)	2
1	medium turnip, peeled and cut into 1 cm (½ inch) cubes	1
5	garlic cloves, coarsely chopped	5
25 g	parsley (with stems), coarsely chopped	¾ oz
10	black peppercorns	10
2	fresh thyme sprigs, or 1 tsp dried thyme	2
2	bay leaves	2

Put the celery, carrots, onions, broccoli if you are using it, turnip, garlic, parsley and peppercorns in a heavy stockpot. Pour in enough water to cover them by 5 cm (2 inches). Slowly bring the liquid to the boil over medium heat, skimming off any scum that rises to the surface. When the liquid reaches the boil, add the thyme and bay leaves. Stir the stock once and reduce the heat to low; cover the pot, leaving the lid slightly ajar. Let the stock simmer undisturbed for 1 hour.

Strain the stock into a large bowl, pressing down lightly on the vegetables to extract all their liquid. Discard the vegetables. Allow the stock to stand until it is tepid, then refrigerate or freeze it.

Tightly covered and refrigerated, the stock may safely be kept for five to six days. Stored in small, tightly covered freezer containers and frozen, the stock may be kept for as long as six months.

Glossary

Allspice: the dried berry of a member of the myrtle family. Used whole or ground, it is called allspice because its flavour resembles a combination of clove, cinnamon and nutmeg.

Arachide (also called peanut or groundnut oil): an oil with a nutty taste containing low proportions of both polyunsaturated and saturated fats.

Arrowroot: a tasteless, starchy, white powder refined from the root of a tropical plant; it is used to thicken purées and sauces. Unlike flour, it is transparent when cooked.

Balsamic vinegar: a mild, extremely fragrant wine-based vinegar made in northern Italy. Traditionally, the vinegar is aged for at least seven years in a series of casks made of various woods.

Basil: a leafy herb with a strong, spicy aroma when fresh, often used in Italian cooking. Covered with olive oil and refrigerated in a tightly sealed container, fresh basil leaves may be kept for up to six months.

Baste: to help brown and flavour a food, and keep it from drying out, by pouring pan drippings or other liquid over it during cooking.

Bâtonnet (also called bâton): a vegetable piece that has been cut in the shape of a stick; bâtonnets are slightly larger than julienne.

Bay leaves: the aromatic leaves of *Laurus. nobilis* — a Mediterranean evergreen — used fresh or dried to flavour stocks and stews; also available in powder form. Dried bay leaves when broken have very sharp edges and can injure internally, so they should be removed before serving.

Blanch: to partially cook food by briefly immersing it in boiling water. Blanching makes thin-skinned fruits and vegetables easier to peel; it can also mellow strong flavours.

Bouquet garni: several herbs — the classic three are parsley, thyme and bay leaf — tied together or wrapped in muslin and used to flavour a stock or stew. The bouquet garni is removed and discarded at the end of the cooking time.

Brown cap mushrooms (also called chestnut mushrooms): a brown-skinned variety of mushroom with a firm texture and a strong flavour.

Bulb fennel: see Fennel.

Burghul (also called bulgur): a type of cracked wheat, where the kernels are steamed and then dried before being crushed.

Calorie (or kilocalorie): a precise measure of the energy food supplies when it is broken down for use in the body.

Cardamom: the bittersweet, aromatic dried seeds or whole pods of a plant in the ginger family. Cardamom seeds may be used whole or ground.

Caul: a weblike fatty membrane that lines a pig's intestines. When wrapped round a lean minced-meat filling, it melts during cooking and moistens the meat.

Cayenne pepper: a fiery powder ground from the seeds and pods of red peppers. Used in small amounts to heighten other flavours.

Ceps (also called porcini): wild mushrooms with a pungent, earthy flavour that survives drying or long cooking. Dried ceps should be soaked in water before they are used.

Chervil: a lacy, slightly anise-flavoured herb often used as a companion to other herbs, such as tarragon and chives. Because long cooking may kill its flavour, chervil should be added at the last minute.

Chili peppers: hot or mild red, yellow or green members of the pepper family. Fresh or dried, most chili peppers contain volatile oils that can irritate the skin and eyes; they must be handled carefully (*see caution, page 36*).

Chinese cabbage (also called Chinese leaves): an elongated cabbage resembling cos lettuce, with long, broad ribs and crinkled, light green leaves.

Cholesterol: a waxlike substance that is manufactured in the human body and also found in foods of animal origin. Although a certain amount of cholesterol is necessary for proper body functioning, an excess can accumulate in the arteries, contributing to heart disease. See also Monounsaturated fats; Polyunsaturated fats; Saturated fats.

Coriander (also called cilantro): the pungent, peppery leaves of the coriander plant or its earthy-tasting dried seeds. It is a common seasoning in Middle-Eastern, Oriental and Latin-American cookery.

Coulis: a sieved vegetable or fruit purée.

Couscous: a fine semolina grain, served with the classic North African stew of the same name.

Crème fraîche: a slightly ripened, sharp-tasting double cream.

Crystal salt: a less refined type of salt than ordinary table salt, suitable for crushing with spices in a mortar.

Cumin: the aromatic seeds of an umbelliferous plant similar to fennel, used whole or powdered as a spice, especially in Indian and Latin-American dishes. Toasting gives it a nutty flavour.

Daikon radish (also called mooli): a long, white Japanese radish.

Dates: the fruit of the date palm, dates can be bought fresh or dried. When dried, choose plump unstoned dates in preference to pressed slab dates.

Deglaze: to dissolve the brown particles left in a pan after roasting or sautéing by stirring in wine, stock, water or cream.

Degrease: to remove the accumulated fat from stock or cooking liquid by skimming it off with a spoon or blotting it up with paper towels. To eliminate the last traces of fat, draw an ice cube through the warm liquid; the fat will cling to the cube.

Dietary fibre: a plant-cell material that passes undigested through the human body, but promotes healthy digestion of other food matter. The fibre in this book is provided mainly by fresh and dried fruits and certain vegetables such as peas and beans.

Dijon mustard: a smooth mustard once manufactured only in Dijon, France; it may be flavoured with herbs, green peppercorns or wine.

Eddoe: a small, potato-like vegetable from South-East Asia and the West Indies with a rough, brown exterior and a nutty flavour.

Escalope: in pork cookery, a thin slice of lean pork usually cut from the fillet, chump end or leg. It is often flattened out and tenderized with a mallet before frying or grilling.

Fennel: a herb (also called wild fennel) whose feathery leaves and dried seeds have a mild anise flavour and are much used for flavouring. Its vegetable relative, the bulb — or Florence — fennel (also called finocchio) can be eaten raw in salads or cooked.

Fibre: see Dietary fibre.

Fillet (also called tenderloin): the most tender muscle in the pig's carcass, located inside the loin.

Fines herbes: a mixture of finely chopped fresh herbs that incorporates parsley plus one or more other herbs, such as chives, tarragon and chervil.

Five-spice powder: a pungent blend of ground Sichuan pepper, star anise, cassia, cloves and fennel seeds; available in Asian food shops.

Fromage frais: a soft, smooth cheese made from skimmed milk. The *fromage frais* used in this book includes a small proportion of added cream and has an 8 per cent fat content.

Fructose: a sugar found in honey and many fruits, fructose is the sweetest of all natural sugars. It can be bought as a powder and looks much like ordinary caster sugar. Since a smaller amount of fructose is needed, the calorie count is reduced.

Galangal: the root of a Chinese plant with a gingery flavour, usually available in ground form.

Ginger: the spicy, buff-coloured rhizome, or rootlike stem, of the ginger plant, used as a seasoning either in fresh form or dried and powdered. Dried ginger makes a poor substitute for fresh ginger root.

Harissa: a fiery-hot North-African condiment, based on red chili peppers.

Hoisin sauce: a thick, dark reddish brown soya-bean-based Chinese condiment. Its flavour is at once sweet and spicy.

Julienne: the French term for vegetables or other food cut into fine strips.

Juniper berries: the berries of the juniper tree, used as the key flavouring in gin. They lend a resinous tang to marinades and sauces.

Kohlrabi: a cruciferous vegetable with an enlarged stem in the form of a light-green or lavender bulb.

Kumquat: a small, bittersweet citrus fruit resembling a tiny orange.

Lemon grass (citronella): a long, woody, lemon-flavoured stalk that is shaped like a spring onion. Lemon grass is available in Asian shops. In powdered form, it is known as Serch powder.

Lemon verbena: a lemon-flavoured herb native to South America and widely cultivated in Europe, available as fresh or dried leaves. In dried form, it is often used to make a herbal tea.

Mace: the dried aril, or covering, that encases the nutmeg seed.

Mange-tout: flat green pea pods eaten whole, with only stems and strings removed.

Mango: a fruit grown throughout the tropics, with sweet, succulent, yellow-orange flesh that is extremely rich in vitamin A. It may cause an allergic reaction in some individuals.

Medallion: in pork cookery, a round or oval-shaped slice of lean pork, for frying or grilling.

Mixed spices: a mixture of spices and herbs, including several of the following: nutmeg, mace, cinnamon, cayenne pepper, white pepper, cloves, ground bay leaf, thyme, marjoram and savory.

Molasses sugar: a soft, moist, dark brown sugar containing molasses.

Monounsaturated fats: one of the three types of fats found in foods. Monounsaturated fats are believed not to raise the level of cholesterol in the blood.

Mozzarella: a soft kneaded cheese from southern Italy, traditionally made from buffalo's milk, but now also made from cow's milk. Full-fat mozzarella has a fat content of 40 to 50 per cent, but lower-fat versions are available. The low-fat mozzarella used in the recipes in this book has a fat content of only about 16 per cent.

Non-reactive pan: a cooking vessel whose surface does not chemically react with food. This includes stainless steel, enamel, glass and some alloys. Untreated cast iron and aluminium may react with acids, producing discoloration or a peculiar taste.

Okra: the green pods of a plant indigenous to Africa, where it is called gumbo. In stews, okra is prized for its thickening properties.

Passion fruit: a juicy, fragrant, egg-shaped tropical fruit with wrinkled skin, yellow flesh and many small black seeds. The seeds are edible; the skin is not.

Phyllo pastry: a paper-thin flour-and-water pastry popular in Greece and the Middle East. It can be bought, fresh or frozen, from delicatessens and shops specializing in Middle-Eastern food.

Pine-nuts: seeds from the cones of the stone pine, a tree native to the Mediterranean. Toasting brings out their buttery flavour.

Polyunsaturated fats: one of the three types of fats found in foods. They exist in abundance in such vegetable oils as safflower, sunflower, corn and soya. Polyunsaturated fats lower the level of cholesterol in the blood.

Prosciutto: an uncooked, dry-cured and slightly salty Italian ham, sliced paper-thin.

Puréed tomatoes: a purée made from skinned fresh or canned tomatoes. Available commercially, but should not be confused with the thicker, concentrated tomato paste sometimes labelled tomato purée.

Quatre épices: French term for a mixture of ground spices, usually pepper, nutmeg, cloves and either cinnamon or ginger. The proportions may vary but the pepper always predominates.

Recommended Daily Amount (RDA): the average daily amount of an essential nutrient recommended for healthy people by the U.K. Department of Health and Social Security.

Reduce: to boil down a liquid in order to concentrate its flavour and thicken its consistency.

Retsina: a Greek wine flavoured with pine resin.

Rice-paper wrappers: brittle wrappers for spring rolls made from rice flour, available from shops specializing in South-East Asian foods. They are softened by dipping them in water.

Ricotta: a soft, mild, white Italian cheese, made from cow's or sheep's milk. The low-fat ricotta used in this book has a fat content of about 8 per cent.

Rocket (also called arugula): a peppery-flavoured salad plant with long, leafy stems, popular in Italy.

Saffron: the dried reddish stigmas of the crocus flower, saffron yields a pungent flavour and a bright yellow colour; available in thread or powdered form.

Salsify: a slender, tapering root, about twice the length of a carrot, with a white or yellowish skin and a faint oysterish flavour. See also Scorzonera.

Saturated fats: one of the three types of fats found in foods. They exist in abundance in animal products and coconut and palm oils; they raise the level of cholesterol in the blood. Because high blood-cholesterol levels may cause heart disease, saturated fat consumption should be restricted to less than 15 per cent of the calories provided by the daily diet.

Sausage casing: Natural casings, stronger than commercial casings, are the cleaned intestines of lamb, pig or ox. Usually sold preserved in brine or dry salt, they can be ordered from butchers or specialist suppliers and should be soaked before use. Lamb casings are generally used for thin sausages, pig or ox casings for thicker ones.

Scorzonera: a thin, long, cylindrical root with brown or blackish skin, very similar in shape and taste to salsify *(see above)*.

Sear: to brown meat by exposing it briefly to very high heat, sealing in natural juices.

Sesame oil: an oil derived from the seed of the sesame plant, frequently used in Chinese cooking.

Sherry vinegar: a full-bodied vinegar made from sherry; its distinguishing feature is a sweet aftertaste.

Shiitake mushrooms: a variety of mushroom, originally grown only in Japan, sold fresh or dried. The dried form should be soaked and stemmed before use.

Shoyu: see Soy sauce.

Sichuan pepper (also called Chinese pepper, Japanese pepper or anise pepper): a dried shrub berry with a tart, aromatic flavour that is less piquant than black pepper.

Smetana: a smooth-textured cultured dairy product made with skimmed milk, used as a low-fat substitute for soured cream.

Sodium: a nutrient essential to maintaining the proper balance of fluids in the body. In most diets, a major source of the element is table salt, which contains 40 per cent sodium. Excess sodium may contribute to high blood pressure, which increases the risk of heart disease. One teaspoon (5.5 g) of salt, with 2,132 milligrams of sodium, contains just over the maximum daily amount recommended by the World Health Organization.

Soy sauce: a savoury, salty brown liquid made from fermented soya beans and available in both light and dark versions. One tablespoon of ordinary soy sauce contains 1,030 milligrams of sodium; lower-sodium variations, such as naturally fermented shoyu, used in the recipes in this book, may contain half that amount.

Star anise: a woody, star-shaped spice, similar in flavour to anise. Ground star anise is a component of five-spice powder.

Stir-fry: to cook cubes or strips of meat or vegetables, or a combination of both, over high heat in a small amount of oil, stirring constantly to ensure even cooking in a short time. The traditional cooking vessel is a Chinese wok; a heavy frying pan may also be used for stir-frying.

Sun-dried tomatoes: tomatoes that have been dried in the open air to concentrate their flavour; some are then packed in oil. Most sun-dried tomatoes are of Italian origin.

Sweet potato: either of two types of nutritious tuber, one with yellowish, mealy flesh, the other with a moist, sweet, orange flesh.

Tabasco sauce: a hot, unsweetened chili sauce. A similar Asian version is the Thai *sriracha* sauce.

Tamarind concentrate: the brown, acidic-flavoured pulp from the seed pod of the tamarind tree, available from Oriental speciality shops.

Total fat: an individual's daily intake of polyunsaturated, monounsaturated and saturated fats. Nutritionists recommend that total fat constitute no more than 35 per cent of the energy in the diet. The term as used in this book refers to the combined fats in a given dish or food.

Tomato paste: a concentrated tomato purée, available in cans and tubes, used in sauces and soups. See also Puréed tomatoes.

Turmeric: a spice used as a colouring agent and occasionally as a substitute for saffron. It has a musty odour and a slightly bitter flavour.

Walnut oil: an oil extracted from pressed walnuts. It should be purchased in small quantities as, once opened, it can turn rancid within a few weeks.

Water chestnut: the walnut-sized tuber of an aquatic Asian plant, with rough brown skin and white, sweet, crisp flesh. Fresh water chestnuts may be refrigerated for up to two weeks; they must be peeled before use. To store canned water chestnuts, first blanch or rinse them, then refrigerate for up to three weeks in fresh water changed daily. Jerusalem artichoke makes an acceptable substitute.

Wild rice: the seeds of a water grass native to the Great Lakes region of the United States. Wild rice is appreciated for its robust flavour.

Worcester sauce: a hot sauce containing vinegar, molasses, chili peppers and tropical fruits and spices. The version used in this book contains no sugar and no added salt.

Index

Picture Credits

Cover: Martin Brigdale. 4: top, Chris Knaggs; bottom left, John Elliott; bottom right, John Elliott. 5: top, Jan Baldwin; bottom left, John Elliott; bottom right, Chris Knaggs. 6: Martin Brigdale. 11-16: John Elliott. 17-18: Jan Baldwin. 19: James Murphy. 20: John Elliott. 21: Chris Knaggs. 22: John Elliott. 23: Chris Knaggs. 24: John Elliott. 25: Chris Knaggs. 26-27: James Murphy. 28: John Elliott. 29: top, John Elliott; bottom, Philip Modica. 30: Chris Knaggs. 31: John Elliott. 32-33: Chris Knaggs. 34: James Murphy. 35: Philip Modica. 36: John Elliott. 37: Chris Knaggs. 38: Jan Baldwin. 39-41: Chris Knaggs. 42-43: Jan Baldwin. 44-45: John Elliott. 46: James Murphy. 47: top, Chris Knaggs; bottom, John Elliott. 48-49: James Murphy. 50: Chris Knaggs. 51: Jan Baldwin. 52: James Murphy. 53: Jan Baldwin. 54: Philip Modica. 55: Chris Knaggs. 56: James Murphy. 57: Philip Modica. 58: Jan Baldwin. 59: Chris Knaggs. 60: James Murphy. 61-62: John Elliott. 63: James Murphy. 64-65: John Elliott. 66-67: Philip Modica. 68: Chris Knaggs. 69-70: John Elliott. 71: Jan Baldwin. 72: Philip Modica. 73: Chris Knaggs. 74: John Elliott. 75: James Murphy. 76: John Elliott. 77: Chris Knaggs. 78: Jan Baldwin. 79: Philip Modica. 80: John Elliott. 81: Philip Modica. 82: James Murphy. 83: top, James Murphy; bottom, Chris Knaggs. 84: Philip Modica. 85: James Murphy. 86: Jan Baldwin. 87: James Murphy. 88: John Elliott. 89: James Murphy. 90: John Elliott. 91: James Murphy. 92-93: Chris Knaggs. 94-95: Philip Modica. 96-97: James Murphy. 98-99: John Elliott. 100-101: Jan Baldwin. 102: John Elliott. 103-105: James Murphy. 106: Chris Knaggs. 107: James Murphy. 108: Jan Baldwin. 109: Philip Modica. 110-111: James Murphy. 112: Chris Knaggs. 113: Jan Baldwin. 114: Philip Modica. 115: James Murphy. 116-117: John Elliott. 118: Philip Modica. 119: John Elliott. 120: Chris Knaggs. 121-122: Philip Modica. 123: James Murphy. 124: Chris Knaggs. 126: James Murphy. 127-129: Chris Knaggs. 130-131: James Murphy. 132-133: Chris Knaggs. 134: John Elliott. 135: Chris Knaggs. 136-137: James Murphy. 138: Chris Knaggs.

Props: the editors wish to thank the following outlets and manufacturers; all are based in London unless otherwise stated. Cover: china, Villeroy & Boch; cloth, Osborne & Little plc; cutlery, Mappin & Webb Silversmiths. 5: platter, (top) Villeroy & Boch; knife, Mappin & Webb Silversmiths. 16: plates, Royal Worcester, Worcester. 17: marble, W.E. Grant & Co. (Marble) Ltd. 19: plate, Royal Worcester, Worcester. 21: platter, Villeroy & Boch. 22: plate, Royal Worcester, Worcester. 26: plate, Villeroy & Boch. 30: plates, Hutschenreuther (UK) Ltd. 36: plate, Royal Worcester, Worcester. 37: plate, Rosenthal (London) Ltd. 38: bowl, Birgit Blitz, Gruiten, Germany. 40: bowl (bottom, left), Arthur Griffiths, The Craftsmen Potters Shop. 42: plate, Line of Scandinavia. 43: plate, Tony Gant, The Craftsmen Potters Shop. 46: (centre, left), David Mellor, marble, W.E. Grant & Co. (Marble) Ltd. 50: plate, Rosenthal (London) Ltd.; cutlery, Mappin & Webb Silversmiths. 52: plate, Villeroy & Boch; cloth, Osborne & Little plc. 53: plate, Hutschenreuther (UK) Ltd.; cutlery and napkin ring, Mappin & Webb Silversmiths; candlestick, Royal Copenhagen Porcelain and Georg Jensen Silversmiths Ltd. 54: bowl, David Mellor; fabric, Osborne & Little plc. 55: plate and vegetable dish, Rosenthal (London) Ltd. 58: platter, Spode, Worcester. 59: plate, Fortnum & Mason; cutlery and wine bottle coaster, Mappin & Webb Silversmiths. 61: Formica, Newcastle, Tyne and Wear; 62: china, Royal Copenhagen Porcelain and Georg Jensen Silversmiths Ltd.; cutlery, Mappin & Webb Silversmiths. 69: plate, Rosenthal (London) Ltd. 70: plate, Royal Worcester, Worcester. 71: plate, Hutschenreuther (UK) Ltd.; peppermill, Royal Copenhagen Porcelain and Georg Jensen Silversmiths Ltd. 72: plate, Rosenthal (London) Ltd.; cutlery, Mappin & Webb Silversmiths. 73: plate, Royal Worcester, Worcester. 74: bowl, David Mellor; napkin, Ewart Liddell. 77: bowl, Mary Rose Hudson. 78: dish, Jenny Clarke, The Craftsmen Potters Shop; marble, W.E. Grant & Co. (Marble) Ltd. 79: bowls, Winchcombe Pottery, The Craftsmen Potters Shop. 80: dish and plate, Wedgwood. 81: plate, Rosenthal (London) Ltd.; cutlery, Next Interiors. 84: cutlery, Mappin & Webb Silversmiths. 87: platter, Hutschenreuther (UK) Ltd; cutlery, Mappin & Webb Silversmiths. 88: plate, Tony Gant, The Craftsmen Potters Shop. 89: fork, Next Interiors. 90: napkin, Ewart Liddell. 92-93: plate, Jane Hamlyn, The Craftsmen Potters Shop; marble, W.E. Grant & Co. (Marble) Ltd. 94: bowl, Mid Wales Development Centre; marble, W.E. Grant & Co. (Marble) Ltd. 98-99: marble, W.E. Grant & Co. (Marble) Ltd. 100: casserole, David Mellor. 101: platter, Villeroy & Boch; knife, Mappin & Webb Silversmiths. 102: plate, Rosenthal (London) Ltd. 104: plate, Villeroy & Boch; napkin, Ewart Liddell. 105: plate and dish, Winchcombe Pottery, The Craftsmen Potters Shop. 106: plate, Thomas (London) Ltd. 108: plate, Line of Scandinavia. 109: plate, Thomas (London) Ltd. 111: rug, Kilkenny; cutlery, Fortnum & Mason; bowl, Tony Gant, Craftsmen Potters Shop. 112: napkins, Kilkenny. 113: plate, Inshop. 115: plate, Hutschenreuther (UK) Ltd.; cutlery, Mappin & Webb Silversmiths. 118: plate, Fortnum & Mason; Formica, Newcastle, Tyne and Wear. 119: marble, W.E. Grant & Co. (Marble) Ltd. 120: platter, Rosenthal (London) Ltd. 122: marble, W.E. Grant & Co. (Marble) Ltd. 124: dish, Arthur Griffiths, The Craftsmen Potters Shop. 126: plate, Villeroy & Boch. 128: platter, Rosenthal (London) Ltd. 132: place mat, Ewart Liddell. 136: plate, Villeroy & Boch.

Acknowledgements

The index for this book was prepared by Myra Clark, London. The editors also wish to thank the following: Rachel Andrew, London; Steve Ashton, London; J. Blackburn, Devon; René Bloom, London; Nora Carey, Hartford, Connecticut; Sean Davis, London; Jonathan Driver, London; Elizabeth David Ltd., London; Richard Guy, Wiltshire; Molly Hodgson, Yorkshire; Isabella Kranshaw, London; Brian Leonard, London; Christine Noble, London; Philomena O'Neill, London; Perstorp Warerite Ltd., London; Katherine Reeve, London; Yen's Roesner, London; Sharp Electronics (UK) Ltd., London; Jane Stevenson, London; Dr. T. Stuttaford, London; Toshiba (UK) Ltd., London; Paul van Biene, London.

Colour Separations by Fotolitomec, S.N.C., Milan, Italy
Typesetting by G. Beard & Son Ltd., Brighton, Sussex, England
Printed in Italy by New Interlitho S.p.A. - Milan